THE
INTERNET
RESEARCH
GUIDE

**A Concise, Friendly, and
Practical Handbook for
Anyone Researching in the
Wide World of Cyberspace**

Timothy K. Maloy

Allworth Press, New York

© 1996 Timothy K. Maloy

All rights reserved. Copyright under Berne Copyright Convention, Universal Copyright Convention, and PanAmerican
Copyright Convention. No part of this book may be reproduced, stored in a retrieval system, or transmitted in any
form, or by any means, electronic, mechanical, photocopying,
recording or otherwise, without prior permission of the
publisher.

Published by Allworth Press
an imprint of Allworth Communications, Inc.
10 East 23rd Street, New York, NY 10010

Cover design by Douglas Design Associates, New York, NY
Book design by Sharp Designs, Holt, MI

ISBN: 1-880559-45-5

Library of Congress Catalog Card Number: 95-83010

Contents

Chapter 8
The Way of the Cybrarian: Making the Internet Meaningful

Chapter 9
Internet Publishing: A Beginner's Guide to Writing HTML

acknowledgements

A project that consumed a great deal of time in becoming familiar with the Net requires some acknowledgments, and they are as follows:

To my father, whom I work with closely in reporting about the Net in our newsletter the *Internet Newsroom*. I have gained valuable insight from his half-century of news experience; in the bargain, he has become a veteran Internet Surfer at seventy-some-odd years old.

To my mother for enduring my father and me as we expanded our media firm, Editors' Service.

To Suzanne Kincheloe, who teaches the Internet to journalists at the National Press Club in Washington, D.C.

To Thomas Timmons, president of Lone Mountain Design and great friend. We first formed an alliance during my nascent print publishing of the now-defunct *Cognitive Coffee Shop* magazine, which we plan to launch again on the Web.

A great debt of thanks to The American University in Washington, D.C. for giving me the opportunity to serve as an adjunct professor in the communications department. By teaching the Internet, I have improved my own scholarship on the subject.

A resounding acknowledgment to those A.U. students who served as my editorial assistants:

- *Adam Steinback:* Began Netsurfing at fifteen and has already launched his own computer consulting firm that specializes in on-line research. He plans a full-time career in the on-line world.
- *Lauren Crowley:* Received her undergraduate degree in communications at The American University and is now pursuing her graduate degree in radio and television there. She is a self-described "Internet Fanatic."
- *Jennifer Sarnelli:* Is currently studying print journalism and political science. Her Internet areas of interest range from the political to the alternative.
- *Greg Micklos:* Has interned for Larry King and "News/Talk 630 AM WMAL." He has also worked in college radio as a talk-show host, news director, and program director.
- *Stacy Olkowski:* Is a journalism/anthropology major at The American University, where she is also a late-night radio show host. A true Victorian in her eclecticism, Ms. Olkowski's interests range from the tropical rainforest to the Internet.

And a grateful thank-you to Mike Weaver of the WebFirst consulting firm, in Chevy Chase, Maryland, for checking technical details.

■

Foreword

One pleasantly balmy November day in 1995, I found myself hard at work in the library of the National Press Club doing Internet-based research. I was borrowing the library's powerful SunSPARC terminal and fast T1 Internet connection in order to look for information about the celebration of Kwanzaa.

Employing my current favorite Internet search engine—known as Excite (http://www.excite.com)—I brought up within forty-five seconds a hypertext listing of information resources about the observance of this celebration. Clicking my mouse at the top of the list, I was jumped immediately to extensive information on the topic.

All within several minutes of starting my search, I knew about when Kwanzaa started, the rituals around it, and most importantly, its meaningful role in the African-American community.

At several other nearby terminals were fellow journalists hard at it, looking for information on politics, international affairs, or perhaps even searching the Web for Washington restaurants to prepare for a festive evening out.

Welcome to the Internet. If we journalists are using this increasingly-popular communications medium for research reasons, then it must be pretty useful. In our profession, you often must become an expert on a topic on short notice. This is called working on deadline.

Barbara Vandegrift, the head librarian, was excited about something. A visitor was expected. I turned around from my research for a moment and there behind me was the visitor: Bill Gates, software mogul, reputed to be one of the richest men in the world.

"This is where we train members of the Press Club in using the Internet," Vandegrift said.

Seeing Gates while Netsurfing was fitting in a way. He is both a product and a cheerleader of the Information Age, and he is in many ways a metaphor for the Internet. With Gates, as with the Internet, it is what's going on inside that matters.

I am fascinated with Gates—a man who has changed the world with his vision of computers for the common man—in the same way I am interested in the some of the other greats of the Information Age.

There's Vinton Cerf, father of the Internet, or Tim Berners-Lee, the chief developer of the World Wide Web.

Or Marc Andreesen, who was the chief creator of the Mosaic and Netscape browsers—all by his mid-twenties. Each of his creations has subsequently led to an explosion of Internet usage and publishing. Andreeson and his Netscape Communications Corporation may come and go, but in the meanwhile he and others are changing the face of the Internet. And in turn, the Internet and its vast store of information—literary, political, scientific, and artistic—will change the face of the world.

Gates, Cerf, Berners-Lee, Andreesen, and others will be looked back on as the early greats of the Information Age, and, like Thomas Edison or Alexander Graham Bell, may seem quaint one day soon. But their creation—the Internet, a.k.a. the Information Superhighway—won't ever seem dated, because it keeps changing and becoming more a part of day-to-day existence with unprecedented speed.

"We become what we behold," wrote media-theorist Marshall McLuhan in 1964. "We shape our tools, and thereafter our tools shape us."

What he said was true of the original Gutenberg printing press; is true of television, and will very soon be true of the Internet.

If information leads to knowledge which in turn leads to power, then the Internet and its future forms will make the common person— you and I—powerful with knowledge of our world and our universe.

Timothy K. Maloy

CHAPTER 1

Meet the Internet

E VER ASK YOURSELF: Why the Internet? Why should I use it? Why was it invented?

The Internet—a vast global network of computers—has become today's hot topic. It has suddenly gone from a somewhat esoteric communication system used by scientists and academics to a household buzzword.

Who hasn't been asked for their e-mail address? Who hasn't been given a lengthy URL address for finding something topical on the Internet?

"Oh yeah, it's on the Web. Just look it up at http://www.blah blah blahh . . ."

Who hasn't heard the joke: "On the Internet no one knows you're a dog"?

What are FTP, Gopher, WAIS, newsgroups, and domain names?

And who hasn't thrown up their hands at some point and said, "What are these people talking about?"

Well, don't worry. When it comes to using and navigating the Internet we are all "Dummies" (as the title of a best-selling

Internet book suggests) in the beginning and even in the middle of developing our skill at using the Internet. It's hard to remember it all, and there are always new things to learn about and from the Internet.

But enough of that.

Why should you as a writer, student, publisher, corporate executive, or information specialist be interested in spending long hours hunkered down in front of a computer screen, surfing through a global computer system? Or put more succinctly:

Why Should You Use the Internet?

The answer is simple. Because the Internet is the "Mother of all Information Sources." You can quote me on that.

Forget (for now) trying to understand the technological workings of the Internet—transfer control protocols and packet-switching networks and all that. What you really need to understand about the Internet isn't so much the technology behind it as what is accessible through the Net.

It is nothing short, in comparability, of the world's biggest library. Through the Net you can visit the majority of the libraries at universities around the world, great and small. And many special libraries are accessible too. Why, even the National Library of Medicine is on the Net. You can also access virtually every federal agency, and many state governments. You can read books courtesy of Project Gutenberg, and you can look at paintings from the Louvre, or the Los Angeles Art Museum, or the Warhol Museum in Pittsburgh, Pennsylvania.

In short, there is information animal, vegetable, mineral, and medical on the Net.

But if the Internet and its World Wide Web is rather like a large (and I do mean large) library—and libraries have always been the collection point for information—what makes the Net different from a standard library? What makes the informational resources available through the Net so special compared with standard library resources?

Whereas traditional types of libraries have individual, separate books, papers, documents, and so forth, the Internet is the equivalent of connecting all the books, papers, journals, and documents together. Besides getting connections (hypertext links) between all the available resources, you also get color pictures, sound, and (very soon) realtime digital movies that accompany the text you read.

The implication of all this on-line information is that you, as a researcher, can immediately access primary source material such as full texts of legislation, congressional debates, recent Supreme Court Decisions, or the U.S. Federal Code almost anywhere, anytime. This goes for a great deal of information from governments around the planet, as well. And there is much international information available from the United Nations.

In Washington, D.C., the Internet alleviates in one stroke much of the need for a physical research presence. This means you don't need to maintain an expensive Washington news bureau or corporate research office (although that has prestige). And you don't have to rely completely on expensive research tools and databases such as Lexis/Nexis.

While this information is actually stored in computer servers at many different geographical locations, the Net allows you to reach out into the world and get this information almost instantly. And it is all interconnected, so by accessing one particular home page on a topic you will often find out about one hundred other home pages that also deal with that particular subject area.

Internet philosopher John Perry Barlow says of this network: "It is rather like the Buddhist notion of Indra's net—an infinite grid of pearls, each of which reflects perfectly the image of every other pearl in it."

All this decentralized communication bodes well for breaking up the office monotony a bit. In fact, with Internet-based research, you don't even need an office. You can use a computer and modem from your study to carry on research from your home. For larger organizations who aren't about to close down their offices, it means you don't always have to send people out into the field for research. Or if you do have staff that is out of the office, they can easily communicate with the office from far afield. And for the individual, the Net presents the possibility of communicating with your office or with the world-at-large from the comfort of home. While this phenomenon—known as telecommuting—is already well known, we may see a lot more of decentralized workforces in the coming years, courtesy of the Internet.

All this can sound like a lot of hype—Information Superhighway and all that. The Internet and the information it makes accessible isn't quite a superhighway yet, as it is often a little too disorganized (which is also what makes it different from a standard library). And for many types of connections, the Net is rather too slow as of this writing to be considered a "superhighway." But, as we will show you, the Internet will prove indispensable to your research, as well as your writing, communications, and even your marketing.

Forget all the hype and hackneyed clichés, and just think of the Internet as the way to read your personal *Encyclopedia Britannica* magnified by a million. (In fact, the *Encyclopedia Britannica* itself is on the net (at http://www.eb.com) as are a number of other famous reference books.)

Think of the Internet as a way to interview sources worldwide via e-mail; think of it as way to connect your staff; think of it also as a way to repackage and deliver much of the print information you already publish.

And, not least, think of the Internet as a way to increase the interaction between you and the world you live in.

Why Was the Internet Invented?

Now that you understand that the Internet is like a vast library, the next thing to understand is that the Internet doesn't really exist.

What?

Well, yes it exists, but it isn't a commercial entity like America Online or CompuServe. There is no one to call and complain to.

No one owns the Internet!

There is no centralized profit motive.

There is no attempt at customer satisfaction.

The Internet is a network of networks. By common consensus it links a myriad computer networks throughout the world who helped create the Internet to improve the transfer of information among each other.

And in the same spirit that universities, libraries, museums, and corporations join the Internet network, they can also leave whenever they want. The present is a golden period in Net history because many different entities are rushing to join, and therefore, there is more information available than ever before.

This is also a unique period because almost everything you access through the Net is free, and that is what differentiates the Internet from commercial on-line services. Right now, for many organizations providing information through the Net, the slogan is "be there or be square." Later on they may wonder if it is worth the cost of giving away information just to be a player. But then, many information publishers of all kinds will eventually find that they can make a lot of money disseminating information through the Internet.

In part, this is dependent on working out a "microtransactions" scheme, whereby an information publisher gets paid every time someone browses their information. Even if a user only pays pennies at a time, which will probably be the going rate, so many people are bound to be using the Net in the future that these pennies could rack up into millions of dollars.

One could conjecture on potential Internet commercial opportunities forever. Some experts believe that the Internet will be the death of the on-line services. And others point to the fact that the "pie" just seems to keep growing in terms of persons going on-line, and that there are enough customers to go around for on-line services and for Internet access providers.

A Bit More Internet History

The Internet had its origins as a computer communications network set up by the Defense Department (DoD). Defense researchers developed something called the ARPA (Advanced Research Projects Agency) Net. It was designed as a computer network that would maintain communications even if individual locations where destroyed by nuclear attack. This was done by using a "suite" of computer communications protocols known as Transfer Control Protocol/Internet Protocols that led to the creation of a decentralized communication system which would dynamically reroute messages around destroyed or disabled sites. This is known as *packet switching*.

NASA and the National Science Foundation (NSF) continued research on this same kind of packet-switching network. The NSF fostered faster communications between its supercomputer centers so that scientists in the U.S. and abroad could make use of supercomputing resources without actually being at a supercomputer center.

This research by DoD, NASA, and the NSF resulted in what has become known by that world-straddling, monolithic noun—the Net.

The growth has been startling. In 1981 there were only about two hundred "host" computers on the Internet. By the beginning of this decade there were 300,000, and in 1995 there were an estimated 3.2 million host computers on the Net.

Until several years ago, the Internet had served largely as a communications medium for academics and scientists—a big inter-office mail system among colleges and universities. Many Net customs come from this academic origin. We will give you a quick lessons in "Netiquette" later on.

The Internet came to popular attention several years ago with the creation of the World Wide Web. European scientists at the European Particle Physics Laboratory (CERN) developed what is known as Hypertext Transport Protocol (http) to allow physicists worldwide to easily exchange and access information.

The subsequent creation of graphical Web "browsers" such as Mosaic and Netscape made the WWW part of the Internet very easy to use, and led to the explosion in Net usage and interest these last several years. These browsers enable Internet users to "read" documents that are on the World Wide Web section of the Net. The interface for the WWW mostly involves "point-and-click" navigation, which is a lot easier than the previous necessity of keyboarding in arcane UNIX commands.

CERN's statement of purpose for the World Wide Web (WWW) is as follows:

> To allow information sharing within internationally dispersed teams and the dissemination of information by support groups. Originally aimed at the High Energy Physics community, it has spread to other areas and attracted much interest in user support, resource discovery and collaborative work areas. It is currently the most advanced information system deployed on the Internet, and embraces within its data model most information in previous networked information systems.

What they don't mention is that the Web is also "cool"-looking, with multimedia documents that can carry text, graphics, and even sound.

And that is it in a nutshell.

Now everybody is jumping on the bandwagon, both in using the Net and in providing information via the Internet. College students routinely access the Internet courtesy of their schools, and they often put up their own personal home pages. Companies are rushing to put home pages on the WWW to act as "electronic storefronts" and information resources. The U.S. government has been reinventing itself by providing comprehensive access to vast amounts of information. And even newlyweds are announcing their new status with Net pages.

Writing in the fall of 1995, a *USA Today* reporter said of all this burgeoning growth: "Welcome to the Internet, an organism unlike any in history."

In the guide which follows, you will find everything you need to know to connect with the Internet and to navigate it successfully. You will discover many of the best sites to visit for a wide variety of research areas and get expert advice on how to use the Internet to find out what you want to know.

■

thousands of domain names for themselves. Kraft, for example, claimed 133 names including hotdogs.com, sanka.com, and velveeta. com. Proctor & Gamble took fifty-two names, including diarrhea.com, luvs.com, metamucil.com, pimples.com, toiletpaper.com, and under-arms.com. Even politicians got savvy after someone registered dole-96.com and set up a satiric Web page. Gingrich, Alexander, Bradley, and Quayle were the first to jump into the registration game.

As the Internet grows, stories like this may abound as everybody tries to claim a stake in cyberspace for themselves. If current growth trends continue, the Information Superhighway will double in size about every one or two years. At this rate, the number of people on-line will equal the world's population in approximately eight years. Chances are growth will level off somewhat before this happens; surely less-developed parts of the world will not grow at the same rate as the United States has.

By 2000, experts agree the majority of people in developed countries will be using the Net regularly. But exactly just who, what, why, where, when, and how these people are using the Internet will be answered by the new cyberdemographers. Recent surveys show on-line activities vary greatly, from playing games, job hunting, using electronic mail, reading novels, or just having fun "surfing" the Net. The challenge for the future will be to qualify who's doing each of these activities and why.

With a solid demographic understanding of the on-line population, the Internet can reach its full potential. More and more companies will become comfortable with the technology and learn how to take advantage of this new medium. Electronic commerce will flourish and bring with it the money and resources needed to make the Internet a truly global and accessible network. As it reaches maturity, the Net will become fully cataloged and mapped, perhaps even replacing the microwave as the most efficient and useful new technology.

For a variety of Internet demographics URLs, point your browser to the following addresses:

- Internet Values and Lifestyles
  http://future.sri.com

- Graphics, Visualization & Usability Center
  http://www.cc.gatech.edu/gvu/user_surveys/

- Matrix Information and Directory Services Internet Demographic Survey
  http://www.mids.org/mids.org/mids/ids2/index.html

- Growth of the World Wide Web
  http://www.netgen.com/infoarea/growth.html

- O'Reilly & Associates, Inc.
  http://www.ora.com/survey

- Survey-Net
  http://www.survey,net

- The University of Michigan Hermes Project
  http://www.umich.edu/~sgupta/hermes/

- YAHOO's Internet Statistics Section
  http://www.yahoo.com/Computers_and_Internet/
  Internet/Statistics_and_Demographics/

CHAPTER 3

Getting Connected

T o start using this global research and information facility, you must first get connected to the Internet. It can be done with a local phone call, and if you are lucky you can obtain access free.

There are three basic methods of hooking up to the Internet: (1) through free public service institutions such as colleges and libraries, (2) through one of the commercial on-line services, and (3) through direct Internet providers.

Free Services

The cheapest way for an individual to plug into the Internet is through a local college, public library, or a so-called FreeNet. The Internet was originally put together, in part, by a consortium of colleges and universities, and they remain among the major users of the service. If you are enrolled in a local or community college, you can probably obtain a computer account from them without charge, and this, in turn, will allow you to get onto the Internet. Even if you are not a student at the college, it will not hurt to inquire about obtaining a computer account from them for minimal cost.

A growing number of public library systems are hooked into the Internet, and if your local library is among them, inquire about accessing the Internet through their computer system. In the state of Maryland, for example, all the libraries are linked to the Internet through a system called "Sailor," which enables Internet access.

In some communities there are Computer User Groups that are tied into the Internet. A membership in the user group can get you onto the Internet at very little cost. There is also a network of "FreeNets" throughout the country, which are organized on a community basis and which provide low-cost Internet access. A later section of this chapter will describe how to find out if there is a FreeNet in your area.

Commercial On-line Services

The easiest way to plug into the Internet is through one of the commercial on-line services; America Online (AOL), CompuServe, the Microsoft Network, or Prodigy. All offer full Internet access to their subscribers, their $10 monthly rates are identical, and all are tied into telephone networks which enable subscribers to connect with a local phone call.

On the plus side, the commercial on-line services are easy to use and provide lots of support to new customers who are learning how to navigate the Internet. They also maintain many other databases which are useful for information seekers. America Online, CompuServe and Prodigy also offer Internet-only service to individuals who don't want their full on-line services, but desire a low-cost Internet access.

On the minus side, accessing the Internet through one of the commercial on-line services is costly if you spend more than a few hours a month Netsurfing. Typically each of the "Big Three" offer five free hours each month to subscribers and after that, surcharges kick in.

Here is a rundown on the big commercial on-line services that provide subscribers with Internet access.

America Online Call 1-800-827-6364 and they will send you a free start-up kit which entitles you to ten hours on-line without charge. After that, the fee is $9.95 monthly for five hours, with additional hours billed at $2.95.

CompuServe Call 1-800-848-8199 to arrange a one-month introductory membership with ten free hours. After that the fee is a flat $9.95 per month, regardless of time on-line. However, you only get three hours on the Internet before a $2.50 hourly surcharge kicks in. They also have an Internet-only service called Spryte which provides three hours on-line for $4.95 monthly.

Prodigy Call them at 1-800-776-3449 to learn about their free, one-month trial membership, which includes ten hours on-line. Regular fees are $9.95 per month for five hours on-line. It costs $2.95 per hour after that.

Microsoft Network When software giant Microsoft introduced Windows 95, it included a new commercial on-line service called the Microsoft Network, which can be used to connect to the Internet. You connect to it directly from Windows 95. Fees are competitive with the other three commercial on-line services.

Internet-Only The three big commercial on-line services—America Online, CompuServe, and Prodigy—began offering Internet-only service to subscribers early in 1996. Customers get low-cost Internet access along with a browser to navigate the World Wide Web. They do not have access to all the databases and other information offered regular subscribers. In return they pay less, generally about $5 per month for three hours on-line, with additional hours costing $2 each.

Direct Providers

The exploding popularity of the Internet has given rise to new business-technocrat entrepreneurs who provide direct access to the global service. There are hundreds of them around the nation and more are starting up each week. They have powerful computer servers and multiple phone lines for subscribers. Cost varies from $15 to $30 per

31

month for unlimited time on the Internet. It's important to deal with a direct provider that you can reach with a local phone call, otherwise your phone bill will go through the roof as you start making heavy use of the Internet.

Direct providers offer two levels of service. The least expensive is a text-based interface, known as a shell account. But take note: it's difficult to navigate in a text-based Internet environment, and one has to learn UNIX commands. The second level of service is graphics-based, like Windows, and gives you pictures and sound as well as text in a pleasing format. You need a graphics-based connection to fully appreciate the vastly-popular World Wide Web section of the Internet.

Direct providers charge about 30 percent more for a graphic interface, and you need a much more powerful computer to fully utilize graphics on the Internet. Check local newspaper advertisements or the telephone Yellow Pages to find local Internet providers. (More about finding an Internet provider later in this chapter.)

Hardware

Almost any computer and modem can be used to connect to the Internet. But as in all things in the computer world, bigger and faster is better.

A bare-bones rig that will enable a you to use the Internet to gather information, contact sources, and tap into government data should include the following: a computer with at least a 486 chip, a 40 to 60MB hard disk, 4MB of memory (RAM), a 14,400 baud modem, and a communications program such as Procomm or Crosstalk. That's enough to let you surf around the Internet in a text-based environment, gather information, send and receive e-mail, and plug into Usenet newsgroups.

If you are addicted to Windows, you will need a more powerful rig, of course. The 486 chip will do the job, but a Pentium would be best. You'll also need at least 4MB of RAM—8MB would be better and 16MB would be best; a bigger hard disk, which will allow you to store more Internet material; and a faster modem.

The bigger, faster machines are a necessity if you intend to access the Internet in a graphics environment. That's because graphics gobble up enormous amounts of memory and hard disk space. And now that the graphics-based World Wide Web is so accessible and popular, we recommend that you go that route.

A stripped-down system will get you on the net, but like a 1960 VW Beetle, an underpowered system will leave you hugging the right-hand shoulder of the Information Superhighway. What we recommend is:

Processor A 486DX is good, a DX2 is better, and a Pentium processor will give you the raw power to handle the large amounts of data from the Web as more entities jump on the multimedia bandwagon.

Hard drive 160MB is minimum, 340 is good, 540+ is best.

RAM 8MB is minimum, 16 is good, 16+ is best (especially for Windows or Mac systems).

Modem 14,400 baud is absolute minimum for access to most commercial on-line services. This is good for a regular dial-up phone line connection and is the minimum for a graphics based SLIP or PPP connection to the World Wide Web. The 14.4 modems can be purchased for under $100, while the 28.8 modems fetch about $200 (though this has been coming down). We suggest making the investment in the 28.8, as you will end up buying one sooner or latter.

Software A basic communications program like Procomm or Crosstalk will allow you to access the Net via a "shell" account. Once you are connected, you will need some other software to navigate. You can download it for free, and we will tell you about navigation later in this chapter.

Finding an Internet Provider

If you are not yet connected to the Internet, or want to shop around for another Internet provider, there's a cheap and easy shopping guide available—but first you'll have to find someone with an Internet connection to access this guide.

It's on the World Wide Web at http://thelist.com. At that location, click your mouse on your local telephone area code and you will be presented with a list of Internet providers in the region and their rates. You can also get a rundown on national Internet providers at that location.

Another way to obtain the information is through The Public Dialup Internet Access List (P-Dial), a compilation of local and national Internet providers which was put together by Peter Kaminski. It is an excellent list, but Kaminski has been slow to update it and you may discover that the only P-Dial list available is one year old.

You can obtain P-Dial by sending an e-mail request to Kaminski, or by downloading it from several sites. For the latest version of P-Dial, simply send an e-mail to info-deli-server@netcom.com and in the body of the message type "Send PDIAL." It will arrive very quickly at your e-mail address. You can also download it, using the File Transfer Protocol (FTP), by going to a number of sites. They include:

- ftp.netcom.com:/pub/info-deli/public-access/pdial
- nic.merit.edu:/internet/providers/pdial
- rtfm.mit.edu/pub/usenet/news/answers/pdial

Several of the commercial on-line services such as America Online and CompuServe also have P-Dial as one of the files you can download in their Internet sections.

In a foreword to his list of Internet Providers, Kaminski notes that phone bills can be a significant part of your Internet costs, unless you make the proper connection. First, check for a provider that is a local call for you, with no long-distance charges. Failing that, compare phone charges for a provider with a 1-800 number or a Public Data Network (PDN) phone number. Some providers will levy a surcharge of up to $9 per hour for 1-800 service. One final note: check the Yellow Pages and local newspaper advertisements for names of any Internet providers in your community.

A Consumer's Guide to Providers

The Internet's soaring popularity for conducting research, making contacts, and conducting interviews makes an Internet connection almost mandatory these days, especially in a metropolitan area. But how do you choose from the multitude of providers? There are several questions you should ask any potential Internet access provider before you write that check, according to respected providers we have interviewed.

Question One: *Who Answers the Phone?* The most important item in determining the worth of a provider is whether or not there is someone available to take your calls during business hours. Services run by answering machine indicate that the business may be a sideline for the owner, which does not bode well for the new user or for those with questions or complaints that must be addressed quickly. Long waits or needing to leave messages because no one is available are also bad signs if they occur regularly. Your provider should also be within your local dialing area.

Question Two: *Which Services Are Offered?* At the very least, you should demand the following services from any provider: electronic mail, Usenet discussion groups, FTP, Telnet, Gopher, Archie, access to the World Wide Web, plus the ability to upload and download files from your home computer. You should also find out how much space your account includes for storing files on the server: 5MB is the most common limit; 2MB is probably not enough.

Question Three: *How Many Phone Lines Are Available?* One of the most common complaints from Internet account holders is the constant busy signal that plagues some providers. Find out the ratio of users to phone lines for each company; 25:1 is good, while ratios of 40:1 or higher greatly reduce your chance of reliably finding an open line. Also find out if the provider can support at least 14.4 kbps modems, though having a number of 28.8 kbps lines is now the de facto standard. Ask about ISDN (Integrated Services Digital Network) connections, and if you're a business, ask about a T1 connection.

Question Four: *How Is the Provider Connected to the Internet?* If system performance is at all a concern, make sure the provider has at least a 256 kbps connection, with either a T1 or T3 line preferred. Also ask what kind of workstation the company uses as its primary server;

if it's a PC, you might want to look elsewhere, as the smaller personal systems can be overwhelmed by loads that are handled easily by the more powerful SparcStation 10s, SparcStation 20s, and HP server lines.

Question Five: *Is Live Technical Support Available, at Least During Business Hours?* A corollary to Question One is the willingness of your provider to help you through the problems you encounter while using their service. You should certainly purchase a basic Unix and Internet reference work (we recommend *The Whole Internet User's Guide and Catalog*, Second Edition), but a provider's willingness to make someone available to answer your questions, handle your comments or complaints, and steady your nerves is a major plus.

Question Six: *What Do You Do to Protect My Privacy?* No system administrator worthy of the name would leave a system open to hackers, but even the most clever techniques can be defeated by a determined attacker. Ensure that your provider does not leave sensitive personal information (such as credit card numbers, phone numbers, or addresses) on the system where it could be discovered. You might also inquire whether the company sells its mailing list to information brokers and what steps need to be taken so that your entry is excluded from the list, if you so desire.

Question Seven: *How Much Does All This Cost?* Assuming that the provider has answered all of your questions satisfactorily, make sure that the price is both reasonable and predictable (no hidden charges). Look for the following items:

- Flat rate, unlimited-time access. Most providers allow their users to stay on-line as long as they care to with no hourly charge, though if the amount of time included per day is sufficient (at least four hours) this requirement may be modified. In the Washington, D.C. area, $20 per month is average for an unlimited-time account, though you can often get discounts by signing up for a year at a time.
- No start-up fee.

- No surcharge for using particular services, especially electronic mail or the World Wide Web.
- A refund or cancellation policy should you move or decide to discontinue your business with this provider.
- A written contract with a system use policy and charging plan explained in plain language.

If all of these questions can be answered to your satisfaction, ask for a trial period of not less than five days so you can test and evaluate the system. If it works as expected, you have probably found the provider for you. Of course, you should stay in touch with the provider to let them know if they are falling short of your expectations, or if they are continuing to provide good access and support.

ISDN Connection

If you want to go first-class, you can connect to the Internet through an Integrated Services Digital Network, or ISDN for short. Essentially, it's a souped-up telephone line (digital vs. analog) which allows Internet connections at about four times the speed of the fast 28.8 baud modems.

An ISDN line is ordered from your local telephone company, and such service will be available in about 70 percent of the country by the end of 1996 (if not earlier). The cost averages $30 per month. There is also a modest cents-per-minute fee charged for actual usage, like making a long-distance call.

If you invest in an ISDN line, you still need an Internet Provider who has the technology to handle such a high speed hookup. You also need several special pieces of hardware attached to your computer, which take the place of your modem.

For this you get faster speed on the Internet. No long waits for graphics-rich pages to load. Swift downloads of data.

37

Cable Modem

Now that you know about the availability and the speed of ISDN lines, you should also be informed that ISDNs and other, slower types of connection may increasingly become obsolete within in a few years because of incredibly fast cable modems.

These type of hookups to the Net promise to deliver the full sci-fi effect of cyberspace that is often written about. For starters, you will be able to get realtime video feeds over the Net, you will be able to order movies from vast data banks, and cable modems will herald the beginning of the first interactive television. But the possibilities aren't limited to just the parochial purpose of watching movies and inter-active TV over the Net. Everything that is accessible over the Internet will be delivered all the faster.

The cable modems undergoing testing currently operate up to a thousand times faster than today's 14,400 bps. Under regular modem speed, for instance, it takes around eighteen hours to download Windows 95 software via the Internet, but with a cable modem this could be done in about one minute.

Several commercial organizations—including Tele-Communications Inc., Time-Warner, Comcast, and Continental Cablevision—are expected to begin offering cable modems during 1996, but their plans aren't yet set in stone. And it will be a while yet until these type of hookups are available across the country.

■

navigating the Internet

O nce you are connected to the Internet, how do you move around in cyberspace? Is it easy or difficult? And how do you find the information you want in this vast library that is not equipped with a card catalog?

The answer to these questions is: It depends on the type of Internet connection you have.

Until 1994, most Netsurfers were computer experts or academics who had "shell" text-based Internet accounts and used complicated commands in the UNIX computer language to get around. But today most new Internet users have a graphics-based account and employ easy-to-use "browsers" to move around on the World Wide Web.

For that reason, we will start this chapter with a description of browsers and how they work. Then we will describe the Internet offerings of the three big commercial on-line services and the browsers they use. We will complete this section with a look at a variety of Internet navigating tools. But first a short note on understanding Internet addresses.

Understanding URLs (Uniform Resource Locator)

For those just entering the Internet, the lengthy Net site addresses that are used can seem a touch confusing. You may ask: Why are they so long? Why are some longer than others? But once you understand how to read and use addresses—URLs in particular—you will be able to navigate the Internet with relative ease and speed.

Any Internet address is comprised of several components. For URLs the part that comes after http:// consists of the host name, often the port number, the directory path, and a file name. The first thing to remember is that the prefix http means that a particular site is located on a World Wide Web server. Here's the URL for the home page of the *Internet Newsroom*, my bi-weekly newsletter publication:

http://www.dgsys.com/~editors/index.html

The host name is /www.dgsys.com/, /~editors/ is the directory path, and index.html is the file name.

By the way: the little "~" is known as the *tilde*, but you don't see it in too many addresses.

Many lengthy addresses you will encounter appear as such because they have a long set of "subpaths" after the original directory path. Here's an example of how to reach the opening lines of *Hamlet* on the Internet, which involves several subpaths:

http://www.mindsprings.com/~hamlet/hamlet/hamlet11.html

The /~hamlet/ is the directory path, and all the "hamlets" after are subpaths to the opening lines.

SCENE I. Elsinore. A platform before the castle.
[FRANCISCO at his post. Enter to him BERNARDO]
BERNARDO   Who's there?
FRANCISCO   Nay, Answer me; stand, and unfold yourself.
BERNARDO   Long live the King!

Gopher addresses can also be expressed in URL form, as appears below for the National Institutes of Health:

gopher://gopher.nih.gov/

In standard Gopherspace (off the Web) you would just type gopher.nih.gov/, without gopher://.

The same goes for File Transfer Protocal (FTP), which can be used as a URL by typing ftp:// and then the address.

■ A Quick Trick with URLs

There's one all-purpose address on the World Wide Web that will give you access to the home pages for numerous companies. The address is:

http://www.name of company.com.

For example: If you insert IBM for "name of company," you will arrive at the IBM home page on the web and find a greeting from Chairman Lou Gestner.

Browsers

To understand the sudden explosion of the Internet and the rapid growth of the Net's most popular area—the World Wide Web—it's necessary to understand the history of Mosaic, the first Web "browser" to come into use.

A browser allows an Internet user to easily access and download the informative multimedia documents available on the World Wide Web. The Web was created in 1991 by scientists at the European Particle Physics Laboratory (CERN, for the French *Conseil Europeén pour Recherches Nucléaires*), and its emergence changed everything.

The Web and the invention of Mosaic as a browser made the unwieldy Internet easy to use. Previously, the only way to navigate this global computer network was by using UNIX commands and sifting through rather unattractive text interfaces. While this text-based interface is often still the faster method of traveling on the Net, the Web has made the Internet easy to use and attractive.

With browsing software such as Mosaic or Netscape, all Net navigators need do is point and click their mice onto highlighted or underlined words (*text links*) that connect them to "documents" which can contain text, graphics, video, and even sound.

In trying to make the Internet easier to use, the CERN programmers created a standard for data and a universal addressing system that led not only to an explosion of Internet usage but also to a huge push toward publishing material of all type on the Internet.

Using commands that are relatively simple, anyone—a company, college, government agency, or newspaper—can publish material in *hypertext* wherein certain parts of a document become a "link" to yet another document. This creates the effect whereby the Web gets its name—a seamless flow of information that is intertwined. The beginning point for any Net travel, and any particular site (corporate or otherwise), is known as a *home page*, and each succeeding link leads to yet more "pages." A browser acts as reader of hypertext language.

It took the invention of browsers such as Mosaic, as a compliment to the World Wide Web, to allow for the point-and-click interface which has become so popular. Mosaic was invented at the National Center for Supercomputing Applications (NCSA) at the University of Illinois in early 1993. After a story ran in the *New York Times* about Mosaic, more than a thousand people a day flooded the Internet to download free Mosaic software made available by NCSA.

While this "client" browser software (in its upgraded version) is still available via NCSA, there are also commercially licensed versions available such as the Mosaic software sold by Spry Inc. under the name "Internet-In-A-Box." All of the World Wide Web browsers are derived somewhat from the original Mosaic software which was written at The University of Illinois. And, each of the three big commercial on-line services—Prodigy, America Online, and Compuserve—now use similar-looking browsers to offer Internet access to their subscribers.

The browsers all have a window that one opens to type in the address, or URL of the World Wide Web site he wants to reach. If you want to get to a location on the Web but don't know the address, there are search tools provided which will look it up for you. Once you find a site you like or find productive, you can add it to a "Hot List" or "Bookmark" on your browser where it can be quickly called up.

The original Mosaic has been superseded by the Netscape Navigator, which was designed by one of the creators of Mosaic. The Netscape Navigator, produced by Netscape Communications Corporation, currently accounts for over 75 percent of the browser software used throughout the Net. Also, the majority of Web pages are designed with

"Netscape enhancement" in mind, which means essentially that they are best viewed and read using Netscape Navigator. But this doesn't mean other browsers are obsolete or no good; there are many out there, and Net surfers should use the one they like best and are most comfortable using.

At the *Internet Newsroom*, we actually use several different browsers depending on our connection—we have connections to the Internet through CompuServe, America Online, Prodigy, and through a private Internet Service Provider (ISP) called Digital Gateway Systems. We don't, however, recommend that everybody get that many connections.

Commercial On-line Services

Now let's examine the Internet offerings of the commercial on-line services. For an individual or office thinking about venturing into the Internet, a subscription to either Prodigy, CompuServe, or America Online is probably the best place to start. The Microsoft Network, which is available to users of Windows 95, is an upstart new commercial on-line service which also offers Internet access.

If you want Internet access, but don't care about the other offerings of the commercial on-line services, you can get a special half-price subscription to America Online, CompuServe, or Prodigy with an Internet-only service. AOL calls its Internet-only service the Global Network Navigator, or GNN. CompuServe's Internet-only service is called Spryte, and Prodigy has not yet given a name to its slimmed-down service.

Here's a rundown on the Internet offerings of the commercial on-line services:

America Online America Online offered a World Wide Web browser to its subscribers in mid-1995. In many ways, the AOL Internet service is the best of the three. The AOL Web browser is fully integrated with its other Internet Services, such as e-mail and Usenet, and is also tied into all of the other departments within the regular America Online service.

Attractive and well-designed, the AOL browser also is faster than those offered by Prodigy and CompuServe, partly because AOL has

43

the new WWW access and fancy, updated graphics face, introduced in the fall of 1995, has brought it even with CompuServe and America Online, its bigger rivals. Prodigy's new Internet-only service will give it another big boost, because the company has obtained a license to use the Netscape browser as the core of the new service. The world's most popular and arguably best browser, Netscape will also be available to regular subscribers to the full Prodigy service.

CompuServe In the spring of 1995, CompuServe became the second of the three big commercial on-line companies to give World Wide Web access to its members. Using technology it purchased from Spry Inc., CompuServe told its 2.8 million members they could plug into the Web at no extra charge, simply by downloading the necessary software.

Currently all three big on-line services have the same fee for basic service: $9.95 monthly for five hours, with extra hours billed at $1.95. Earlier, each of the three had also provided such other Internet services as e-mail, Gopher, Usenet newsgroups, and Telnet.

The new CompuServe World Wide Browser runs under Windows and is actually the Spry Mosaic browser, which is familiar to anyone who previously purchased Spry's popular $99 "Internet-In-A-Box" package. CompuServe acquired Spry in March of 1995.

To use the Browser, CompuServe customers are provided with a special "NetLauncher," which is simply the Spry telephone dialer which connects customers to the Web. Subscribers must have a 386 or higher computer and a modem with a speed of at least 9,600 bps. CompuServe said it is converting its entire network to handle speeds of up to 28.8 kbps.

The CompuServe browser has the usual features, and includes a system which first loads text for a user to read, and then loads graphics, which take longer. Unlike the systems used by Prodigy and America Online, CompuServe subscribers must exit the Web browser and return to the regular CompuServe service in order to use Gopher, FTP, Telenet, Usenet, and other Internet features as well as the regular CompuServe offerings.

The Microsoft Network Newest of the commercial on-line services is the Microsoft Network, which is bundled with Windows 95. Fees are similar to the other services, and there is the option of using the Microsoft Network to get onto the Internet at no extra charge.

The Microsoft browser is well designed and fast. The opening home page has several excellent menu choices, and one of them is an Internet Tutorial for individuals who are new to cyberspace. The best link on the page is one in the center labeled "Explore the Internet." It takes users to a page similar to that offered by the Web sites of the other commercial on-line services. There is a "Search" label which connects you to either the YAHOO, InfoSeek, or Excite search engines. The "Reference" link has links to lots of on-line data. Microsoft also leads users to its own daily list of favorite Web pages.

navigation Tools

Now that it's so easy to get on the World Wide Web, not many Internet users will be sticking with simple, lower-cost, text-based connections to the Net (they're not that much cheaper). But for those who prefer the speedy text-based Internet connections—which are not weighed down by slow-loading graphical material—here are some of the basic navigation tools.

Gopher The Gopher is an Internet search tool that was developed at the University of Minnesota, where the state animal is the gopher and the school mascot is the "Golden Gopher." As an Internet utility, Gopher is aptly named after a burrowing rodent because it is great way to cut through a lot of Internet red tape and go directly to your destination.

Your Internet provider should have Gopher software running and listed as one of the available menu choices. If not, download it from The University of Minnesota. Use FTP to get to boombox. micro. umn.edu, then go to the /pub/gopher directory to find the software.

When you are using Gopher, you need to know the address of the Gopher site you want to visit. For example, if you type gopher marvel.loc.gov, you can burrow into the Library of Congress MARVEL system.

There are nearly 7,000 Gopher sites around the world. (To get the list, type telnet infoslug.ucsc.edu, hit Enter, and you'll have a menu from The University of California at Santa Cruz. Select "The World" from the menu and a new set of menus categorizes and lists all the Gopher sites and their Internet addresses.)

Moving around on Gopher menus is easy. Move your cursor to the menu selection you want, or type its number and hit Enter. To get to the next page of a menu, press the space bar; to go back to the previous page, type "b"; to go up to the previous menu, type "u."

For a demonstration of how Gopher works, here is how we used it to obtain crime information and statistics from the United States Department of Justice. We logged onto the Net, and at the UNIX prompt—which in our particular shell account is a dollar sign ($)—we typed the word "gopher" followed by a space and the Department of Justice Internet address: justice2.usdoj.gov. We hit enter and the following menu appeared:

Internet Gopher Information Client v1.11
Root gopher server; justice2.usdoj.gov

1. Welcome to the Justice Department Gopher Server
2. What's new on the Justice Department Gopher Server
3. CRS Information Center Numbers for Cuban Detainees at Krome
4. Justice Department Administrative Documents
5. IGNet
6. IGNet (New and improved, but under construction)
7. Antitrust Division
8. Civil Rights Division
9. Federal Bureau of Investigation
10. Internet Gopher Sites
11. Justice Department Attorney Job Listings
12. Office of Information and Privacy
13. Office of Justice Programs
14. Office of Public Affairs
15. Requests for Proposals

Select any one of these menu choices and hit Enter. You will be confronted with another detailed menu listing all kinds of information. Item number 13, Office of Justice Programs, lists eighteen choices, ranging from "Census of Law Enforcement" to "Crime Statistics 1990."

Item number 5, the IGNet, refers to the Inspector General's office, and accessing it yields seventeen menu choices. They include access to numerous IG reports, the IG audit library, and material from various state Inspector General offices.

The Justice Department Gopher site is chock-full of crime data. For example, we did a *keyword* search in the Bureau of Justice Statistics. The keywords we used were "uniform crime report," and up popped eighteen lists of crime statistics; federal, state, and local. It was heaven for a crime reporter wanting to put his local story into some kind of perspective.

But the main menu entry for "Justice Programs" is where you will normally start your hunt for criminal justice facts and figures. Bring your cursor alongside "Justice Programs," then hit Enter—and yet another menu will appear that offers an option for "Bureau of Justice Statistics." Bring your cursor alongside this entry, then hit Enter. A menu with over seventy different statistical offerings—ranging from prison and police statistics to murder and rape reports—will appear.

Now make your choice from this menu of the type of statistics useful to what you may be researching. Once you have the statistics you are looking for you can either use the Print Screen key to have them printed out on your printer, or you can "mail" the data to yourself via the Internet. For electronic mail, type "m," at which point you must type your e-mail address. The file you are viewing will send itself to your electronic mailbox. Or, you can transfer files to your computer using the File Transfer Protocol (FTP), which we will explain in the next section.

Now that we have told you how to access the U.S. Justice Department with Gopher, it is only fair that we tell you that the whole process is much easier if you utilize the World Wide Web to reach the Justice Department home page. All the same information is there, and it is much easier to get using the point-and-click hypertext language. In fact, during the last half of 1995, all the major federal agencies created Web home pages that also contained Gopher menus of information which were previously only available in Gopherspace.

To get to Gophers on the Web, you use a Uniform Resource Locator such as this one for The University of Minnesota where Gopher was invented:

gopher://gopher.micro.umn.edu/

At this Internet address you will find a gateway to literally "All the Gophers in the World," with breakdowns for continents and countries. There is also a large subject directory.

A few other "Good Gophers" URLs include the following:

- The Electronic Newsstand
  gopher://internet.com

- The Library of Congress
  gopher://marvel.loc.gov

- Wiretap (A place loaded with electronic text ranging from the classics to hip, new on-line journals)
  gopher://wiretap.spies.com/

File Transfer Protocol The Gopher is great for going places, but a practical Net Surfer must know the ins and outs of the File Transfer Protocol (FTP) to access and transfer files from other computers to your own.

If you are using a text-based "shell" Internet account, FTP sites throughout the Net allow you access everything from software to census data. With FTP you can search through computer directories on a global scale.

If you are logged onto the Net and want to travel to a useful File Transfer Protocol site, you either type "FTP" after the UNIX prompt or choose "FTP" from the menu of options that your Net access provider offers. At the next prompt, type the FTP address that you want. For example, the address of the Pentagon's Network Information Center is nic.ddn.mil, so when you are logged onto FTP you type that address. When you arrive at the Department of Defense (or any other FTP site) you will be asked to log on and for your password. Log on as "anonymous" (hence the name Anonymous FTP) and give "guest" or your e-mail address as the password.

To find the file you want, first get a list of directories by typing "ls," select the directory you want, and again type "ls," and a list of filenames will appear. (If it's not in the first directory you search, type "cd" to change directories.) When you spot the file you want, type "get" and the name of the file. If you want several files, type "mget."

The files will be transferred at lightening speed to your directory back at your Net provider. Your provider will have a menu choice that will enable you to download the file to your own computer.

In file names, you must use the upper and lower case letters precisely as they appear on the screen, because FTP is "case sensitive." If you mix up your upper and lower cases, the file transfer will fail.

Your transfer will take place in two parts: FTP first sends the file to your Net provider, and then you download it to the safety of your own computer.

Each of the three big commercial on-line services offers the FTP utility, and they make it a lot easier to use than is the case with an Internet shell. If you want to download an Internet file, you simply use the FTP section offered by the on-line service, and no special UNIX commands are required. The service dumps the file into a special "download" directory in your computer where you have immediate access to it.

Here are just a few top FTP addresses that you can use to access and download various files.

- Internet Information Hunt: This is a "how to" for finding information on the Net and comes complete with examples.
  ftp.cic.net/pub/hunt/about/

- A Net-Guide:
  ftp,cni.rog/pub/net-guides/i-hunt

- CERN: The Nuclear Particle Physics Laboratory—Birthplace of the Web
  info.cern.ch/pub/www

- Project Gutenberg: This is the FTP directory of the project that hopes to make many of the world's book available via the Net.
  ftp.src.doc.ic.ac.uk/Project-Gutenberg

- Wiretap Classics: This is a Net locale that has classic books available.
  wiretap.spies.com/Library/Classics/

- Windows Software:

    sunsite.unc.edu/pub/micro/pc-stuff/ms-windows

    or:

    garbo.uwasa.fi/pc/windows

Telnet In an age of broad Netscapes and beautiful Mosiacs, an old workhorse like Telnet may seem hopelessly tired. Yet we frequently use Telnet to log onto some sites that are very useful to information professionals. The purpose of Telnet is to operate one computer from another, remote computer.

Telnet is set up as a client-server program. The client must be loaded on the computer you are using and the server component loaded on the remote computer you want to use. If you have a text-based UNIX shell account, your Internet provider usually will have Telnet as one of the choices on the opening menu. If your have a graphics-based SLIP or PPP account, you must have Telnet loaded into your own computer. Most of the commercial on-line services, and packages such as Internet-in-a-Box, include Telnet.

After selecting Telnet on the menu or the Telnet icon in a graphics environment, the first step in Telnetting is to type in an address. Typically one types remote.computer.name at the Telnet prompt. For example, to get to Library of Congress computer, type locis.loc.gov.

We find the Library of Congress a highly useful and relatively easy to use Telnet goldmine. Simply by Telnetting there, we have been able to do extensive research on federal and foreign legislation, access the Library of Congress Catalog, access copyright information, or search an organization database.

Since we use these databases frequently, it saves considerable time to Telnet directly to the computer of the Library of Congress rather than going through a Gopher or other Internet browser. There are a great many Telnet sites like the Library of Congress which are highly useful to information professionals.

Now that I have told you how useful Telnet is, let me warn you about a few problems. Telnet is very vulnerable to network traffic. It frequently happens that your Telnet session seems to freeze or get hung up. It may be best to simply escape from the hung session and begin again. When you first connect to a remote computer, they usually tell you the escape character, which is frequently shown as a control character and square bracket ^]. So the escape sequence is to press Control and] at the same time. After typing the escape sequence, type "quit" and your Telnet connection should close.

After you have entered an escape, you can also type "?" to get a list of all the commands available. Here is a list of standard Telnet commands:

TELNET COMMANDS

close	current connection
display	operating parameters
mode	try to enter line by line or character-at-a-time mode
open	connect to a site
quit	exit Telnet
send	send special characters (send ? for more)
set	set operating parameters (set ? for more)
status	print status information.
toggle	toggle operating parameters (toggle ? for more)
z	suspend Telnet
?	print help information

These commands can be important, because Telnet can become frustrating. Because of the way computer terminals developed historically, there are still several different standards on the network. You may run into an IBM system running on the VM or VMS operating systems, or a Sun system using SunOS. Using ordinary Telnet with such systems results in the message that the connection is terminated or refused by the remote host. In such a case, you can try typing "tn3270" to connect to IBM systems or "rlogin" for UNIX. With the commands listed above and a good deal of trial and error, you may be able to connect with recalcitrant remote computers.

Despite these problems and the increasing attractions of parts of the Net like the World Wide Web, Telnet continues to be one of the major tools for Internet researchers. Effective Telnetting requires some investment in time and practice. The great advantage of Telnet, however, is that it can bring significant time savings to researchers under deadline pressure, especially when they have kept a log of valuable Telnet sites.

UNIX The Internet employs a computer language called UNIX. There's no reason to understand UNIX, but you do need to know some of the commands so you can navigate Internet in a text-based mode.

When you first enter UNIX on the Internet you will be greeted by a dollar sign ($) which is the UNIX prompt. Think of it like the DOS prompt you get when you boot up your computer. All you do is enter commands at the $, and UNIX will carry out your wishes.

If you want to list the files in the opening directory simply type "ls" and the directory files will appear.

To change directories type "cd."

To display text from a file, type "more" and you will see a screenful of data. Hiting the spacebar once will display the next screenful of data. Typing "b" will take you back one page.

To print a file, type "lpr."

To return to the UNIX prompt, type "q."

To get out of UNIX, type "exit."

UNIX also uses control commands, which are invoked by holding down the Ctrl key and then typing a letter. Ctrl-z will cause a program to pause, Ctrl-c will kill a program while Ctrl-u will undo a command.

Once you start roaming around the Internet, you will come across various "Help" screens where you can download lengthy lessons on UNIX.

Other Internet Features

While the Internet is justly renowned as a vast information repository, it also has other attractions. This section will deal with three of them, e-mail, Usenet, and Listserv.

E-Mail

One of the most basic tools for individuals using the Internet is e-mail, and it can be one of the most valuable for researching.

Electronic mail has long been used outside of the Internet for inter-office communication, but the growing popularity of the Internet has caused the use of e-mail to explode out of the office.

Nowadays, those with Internet access send e-mail between cities, states, countries, and indeed, whole continents. For instance, we at the *Internet Newsroom* routinely receive e-mail subscription inquiries from such places as Australia, the UK, and Scandinavian countries. We can respond for the same cost as sending an e-mail across town—nothing!

We do pay $25 monthly to our Internet provider for Internet access, but once on the Internet everything is essentially free. In the case of Internet e-mail there is no cost, because what one is actually doing is sending the mail to a provider who then sends it to yet another computer, and so on until it travels the linkages of the Internet and arrives at its destination across the street or around the globe.

There are many ways to use e-mail. Say you need to contact your U.S. government representative with a request for help, or to express your opinion on pending legislation. It's likely he or she has an e-mail address. This enables you to send e-mail to a busy congressional staff secretary; your query or opinion and a response could show up an hour later. Similarly, e-mail queries can be sent to a variety of other state and federal offices with a request that they respond by e-mail.

If you don't know the e-mail address of the public official or the government office, that's no problem. There are several programs that one can utilize to locate e-mail addresses.

But to be frank, often the best way to find out an e-mail address—particularly one you may use fairly often—is to call the person or office in question. It's just plain quicker.

Sending and receiving e-mail is easy, provided that you have Internet access. Most Internet access providers, as well as commercial on-line services such as CompuServe, America Online, Prodigy, and the Microsoft Network supply their customers with an easy-to-use mail manager programs.

These managers allow you to compose and address e-mail at your leisure off-line, and then send them with the press of a key when you go on-line. The mail manager alerts you that you have waiting mail when you sign on and makes it easy to read and respond to that mail by typing your reply and hitting a key. The address for the reply is automatically affixed.

It will help, however, if you understand how to read and translate Internet e-mail addresses.

For example, my personal e-mail address is:

timmaloy@aol.com

My address encompasses my name and where I'm at: America Online (the "@aol" part). The "where I'm at" in any e-mail address is known as the *domain*.

The address of Editor's Service, our newsletter publishing company which produces the *Internet Newsroom*, is:

http://www2.dgsys.com/~editors/

In this case, the .dgs stands for Digital Gateway Systems, our Internet provider and also the domain in this address. Within the domain of an address is something called the *zone*, which in this case is .com. "Com" means that the DGS domain is in the commercial zone of the Net.

Here is a further breakdown of domain zones which can be used for reading and uderstanding both e-mail addresses and URL addresses.

EDU will be found in all e-mail addresses emanating from university origins. The EDU stands for *educational* institutions. An example is harvard.edu.

GOV Stands for any U.S. *government* site such as nih.gov for the National Institutes of Health.

MIL This is the designation (can you guess) of any *military* site on the Net. Prudent hackers will often avoid fooling around anywhere on the Net that has either a .gov or .mil.

ORG Stands for *organization* and includes a number of groups who may not come under the above designations.

Usenet

Usenet Newsgroups are not about news as such; rather, they are affinity groups. There are thousands of them, and they are among the most popular features on the Internet. Often the Usenet and its individual newsgroups are referred to as the "public square" of the Net. Other analogies compare them to a "tavern" gathering of like minds.

The prefixes for the various Newsgroups gives a clue as to the area of interest, as in "rec" for recreation-hobbies, "comp" for computers, and "alt" for any so-called "alternative" group, which are groups organized along somewhat informal lines. One example is alt.journalism, where newsies hang out and chew the fat. Another is alt.tasteless where people discuss, well, "tasteless" jokes, pranks, and related phenomena. The "alt" category is also home to the more "racy" groups such as alt.sex.bondage.

One of my early favorites when I first plunged into the Usenet was alt.coffee, where the chatter was all about the coffee explosion—particularly with regards to coffeehouses—all across America, and indeed the world. For instance, I was going to Dublin, Ireland, and wanted to find out about coffeehouses there; so I posted an "article" to the group about this topic and got a number of quick replies.

Incidentally, in keeping with the "news" metaphor for these newsgroups, sending message to a group is called "posting an article." As a journalist, I was initially confused at what I thought was a misuse of terminology, but then concluded, "What the heck, when in Rome . . ."

Other prefixes for Newsgroups include: "comp" for discussion of computer and computing information; "sci" for, yes you guessed it, science discussions; "soc," which is the prefix for groups devoted to the discussion of social issues, as in "sociology."

As mentioned for the "alt" groups, each of these categories then has sub-hierarchies of discussion. For example, within the "soc" groups there are such breakdowns as soc.culture.hongkong, or soc.culture.india, or soc.feminism. And this is by no means an exhaustive list.

Under computer groups you will find such groups as comp.lang which is devoted to discussions of computer languages; even more specific is a group such as comp.unix wherein members discuss UNIX.

We could go on, but we won't. I trust that you get the basic idea of how these groups are designated. Depending on your individual area of interest, the Newsgroups are like attending a convention of experts every day.

A complete new users introduction and orientation to the Usenet is available at news.announce.newusers. Start with "A Primer" and

"What Is Usenet" and progress to "Emily Postnews" and "Answers to Frequently Asked Questions." A note about this: at almost all news-groups and at many other Internet sites, there is a section called the FAQ (frequently asked questions), which it is always particularly helpful to read.

As far as access goes, the majority of Internet service providers (ISPs) give members a gateway to the Usenet and the thousands of News-groups therein. To read the "postings" to the Newsgroups, you will need a "newsreader," which is often part of the Internet browser software that is currently being sold. You can also get newsreader software separately from a browser. When choosing a potential Internet service provider, ask them about their Usenet access and about software for reading and posting messages to the Newsgroups.

Quick Tip If you want to quickly research topical "postings" to Usenet newsgroups, the Deja News Query Service is one of the foremost Internet search engines for doing across-the-board searches throughout the Usenet.

You can do a keyword search for topical postings (i.e. "Clinton and Sex Scandals") and also search for names and even check postings according to e-mail addresses in order to look in on who is saying what about whom. And Deja News enables you to search through a full year's worth of postings.

Deja News will give you the full text of any relevant posting that it comes up with. To utilize this particular search capability, go to this URL: http://dejanews2.dejanews.com.

Another Tip Besides going to the "news.announce.newusers" news-group to read the Frequently Asked Questions (FAQs) and learn about newsgroups in general, you can go a very helpful Web site at Ohio State where there is a vast compilation of FAQs for thousands of individual newsgroups. These different FAQs answer all the frequently asked questions that pop up in the different newsgroups, and they are a goldmine for researchers who want subject area information. Whether you want to know more about how the Tarot works or are doing a research paper on what the caffeine level is for different types of coffee, you can find the answers at this Internet address: http://ww.cis.ohio-state.edu/hypertext/faq/usenet.

Here's an example of a FAQ answer about the 1996 Summer Olympics in Atlanta that I found through the above Web site that deals with Usenet FAQs (found at: http://www.cis.ohio-state.edu/hypertext/faq/usenet/1996-olympics-faq/faq.html).

> Marathon, Race Walking, Road Cycling are free, if you can find a place to stand by the roadside.
>
> How do I get tickets?
>
> Tickets went on sale May 1, 1995. The plan in the U.S. is to distribute order booklets at retail outlets such as McDonalds and stores that sell Coca-Cola. Forms can now be obtained by sending $5.00 to ACOG, 1996 Ticket Request Form, P.O. Box 105153, Atlanta, GA 30348-5153. Orders placed before June 30, 1995 for "oversold" events will be put into a lottery pool to determine who gets tickets. People who ordered tickets should find out in early September what tickets you were able to get. If you were not able to get the tickets you ordered, you must request a refund from ACOG or they will keep it as a "contribution." Tickets will no longer be available by mail after December 1995.

Listservs

A Listserv mailing list is an e-mail–based discussion group composed of people interested in a specific subject or topic of discussion. Instead of sending an e-mail to a particular individual on the mailing list, messages are sent to a Listserv address. Then each message is automatically distributed to everyone who subscribes to the list.

Subscribing to a Listserv requires that you have an e-mail address and a genuine interest in the topic of discussion. If you subscribe to several active Listservs, you will find your e-mail mailbox full of messages every day. If it turns out the Listserv members are discussing items of little or no interest to you, simply send an e-mail unsubscribing to the Listserv.

Many Listservs are organized along professional lines. There are Listservs for accountants, lawyers, small-business owners, even journalists. To subscribe to one of these Listservs, send an e-mail message addressed to the *node* (not the e-mail address) which manages the list. Use the form listserv@hostname. The body of the message should be in this form: "subscribe (your first and last name)." For example, there is a Listserv dealing with computer-aided news reporting. Its name is CARR-L, and the host name is ulkyvm.louisville.edu. To subscribe you would send an e-mail to: listserv@ulkyvm.louisville.edu.

The message on your e-mail should read: "subscribe CARR-L (your first and last name)."

A note on netiquette

The word Netiquette is simply an amalgam of "Net" (short for Internet) and "etiquette" (as in how to behave appropriately). And thus you may view Netiquette as a set of simple rules for behavior on the Information Superhighway to ensure you don't come across as an idiot.

The most basic rules of Netiquette are those regarding the use of e-mail, Usenet, and Listservs, and essentially pertain to writing or posting things that don't reflect badly on you. So here goes:

- Remember that while e-mail is private, it can be re-posted with ease. So don't write anything you don't want floating around to someone who will re-post it (i.e. don't send an e-mail knocking the boss to an office mate that your "mate" might re-post, getting you in trouble. The same applies to love letters and other missives—think twice about what you say and to whom you are sending it).
- In the same vein, remember that e-mail can be mislaid, as it were, and become the focus of public scrutiny. Remember that on the Usenet and within Listservs, you are in essence interacting in a public space. If you wouldn't shout something nasty on the street corner, then don't do it in cyberspace either. Again, watch what you say, whom you say it to, and whom you are saying it about.
- For most e-mail and Usenet/Listserv postings, keep your message short. Some folks insist on rewriting *War and Peace* on the Net. Considering the amount of e-mail everyone receives these days, it is rude to make people read overly long messages.
- In this same spirit, keep your publicity/advertising efforts using e-mail, Usenet, and Listservs to a minimum. If you post ob-

viously commercial messages (i.e. "Well-Made Decoy Ducks For Sale") in the wrong places, you will get laughed at, or even worse, *flamed* (see glossary).

• All the above established: Go ahead and relax and enjoy yourself. People often let down their hair using e-mail, Usenet, and Listservs, and this informality is a good thing. But when you are cruising around the Internet just being yourself, remember that courtesy is a good habit—in cyberspace and elsewhere.

■

CHAPTER 5

Researching on the Internet

What are the research methods in a traditional library? You might go to the *Readers Guide to Periodical Literature* or the card catalog, you will probably consult the reference librarian, and you will probably also simply browse the stacks.

Most information in a library is broken down into books, periodicals, and audio-visuals, with categorized references available as to where information can be found.

Well, on the Internet, finding things is a little bit different.

A General Approach to the Net

Many people compare the Internet to a very large library. Still others qualify this analogy by calling the Internet a "library without a librarian," as a way to describe its inherently chaotic organization. But in understanding how to use the Internet for research, it is important to know that while the Internet is like a library, it cannot always replace a library.

The Internet is among the top methods for researching

almost any subject, but the Net should not serve as your exclusive method of research. Instead, the Net should serve as but one arrow—one of your most deft—in your entire quiver of research methods, traditional and otherwise. Put simply: You can find an enormous amount of information on the Internet, but you should also supplement that with a trip to a traditional library, depending on how thorough the scope of your research is.

One common question that arises from the library analogy is when or whether all books and articles that appear in print will be digitized and placed on the Internet. In fact, it is highly unlikely that printed books and articles will be offered digitally on a comprehensive scale within the very near future. Copyright issues and the difficulties of Internet commerce currently riddle the wholesale access of print materials. Some articles from magazines are available on the Internet, as are many books that have outlived or never had the privilege of copyright. But the text and graphics of entire newspapers and current books are not always available, at least for now.

Still another school of thought would argue that simply transferring print materials to digital formats does not do justice to either the printed or electronic media. The hypertext capabilities of the World Wide Web have created a huge demand for content that is unique to the on-line environment. In most fields outside of computer science and popular culture, the content is spotty, in some cases experimental, and is generally regarded with caution. It is no accident that the most trusted content on the Internet is that which has its original source in some other media—a printed article or government document, the transcript of a broadcast, and the like.

The upshot of this is that the Internet is no substitute for a traditional library, but an enhancement or supplement to an overall research strategy. The first rule of any kind of research is "garbage in, garbage out," meaning that one's research is only as good as the tools one uses and the comprehensiveness and objectivity of one's search. This chapter will show how the Internet is best used as a component in an overall research strategy.

Here are some thoughts on areas where the Internet is particularly strong:

- Good for access to government documents and publications that are either difficult to find or simply unavailable from one's local library.

- Special on-line versions of traditional print materials—EDGAR (Securities and Exchange Commission company information), *Encyclopedia Britannica*, THOMAS (Library of Congress), Congressional Record, Electronic Newsstand—offering reprints of some (but not all) articles from major periodicals.
- Unique materials available only on the World Wide Web— software and shareware, electronic journals, and hypertext versions of periodicals (UTNE Online, NBC, CNN, etc.) that feature different content than their traditional-media counterparts.
- Press releases, and media contacts—the Internet is a vast source of "unmediated" news.

(In the directory section, we provide Internet addresses (URLs) for all the above resources.)

Ten Tips for Internet Researching

Because expectations of the "Information Superhighway" can get easily overblown by hype and news media reports or by advertising that exaggerates the ease of Internet usage, you should keep a level head when approaching the Net. And as in any other research endeavor, you should adopt a formal strategy to maximize results. Here are some tips that are commonly suggested for starting your Internet research:

1. Ask yourself, your client, or your boss: Exactly (as close as possible) what is the information that is being looked for? Is it legal, scientific, literary, or artistic? Is the topic animal, vegetable, mineral? What is the subject category? Who may be the author of what you are looking for? What is the date of publication? Is the material from a book, magazine, scientific paper, or abstract? Are you looking for an electronic publication or a paper publication that also may exist in digital form on the Net?

2. While finding particular information on the Internet is exactly what you are trying to attempt, do you already know that this information is indeed somewhere on the Internet? Have you heard or read that it is on the Net? Did your boss say it is on the Net? (Finding out as much as you can about exactly where on the Internet it may reside makes it that much easier to find.) Did you previously run across a certain resource during earlier Internet research that you are now trying to track again?

3. In the same vein as both of the above: What keyword or keywords might help you find what you are looking for? (Use of keywords is described more extensively in the next chapter, about Internet search engines.)

4. As much as possible, familiarize yourself with what resources and organizations are on the Internet. There are a number of Internet-based and hard-copy directories (including one in this guide) that cite specific resources. With regards to Internet-based directories, there are a number of top spots to begin your research. For instance, we will later tell you about YAHOO, which as of this writing is one of the premier Internet directory resources.

5. Also, to stay current in your subject area and familiarize yourself with what's out there, you should join relevant subject-related Listserv (mailing list) groups and Usenet groups. As we mentioned in earlier sections on both of these resources, there are thousands of them to pick from and they cover nearly every subject imaginable, from biology to body piercing. Also there are a variety of electronic newsletters, such as Gleason Sackman's "Net Happenings Digest" that publishes new sites categorized by topic on a continual basis.

6. As you familiarize yourself with the Net, start "bookmarking" your favorite and most helpful research home pages. The bookmark function is contained in all Web browsers and allows the Net surfer to compile a list of Net addresses so he or she can return to this list with a "point-and-click" for reference purposes. For example: If you often research using U.S. Government information, then you would want to book-mark THOMAS, the Internet guide to the government, hosted by the Library of Congress.

7. After you have familiarized yourself with the myriad of informational resources on the Internet and are quite knowledgeable about all the different Internet guides and search engines, you should maintain a high degree of discipline when researching—remember to stick to the topic you are looking for. With an estimated 80 million pages on the World Wide Web portion of the Internet alone, it is easy to find yourself sidetracked as you are led down the garden path away from your original topic. The Internet is Victorian in its eclecticism; that is both its beauty and its danger. So stay focused and don't wander from Civil War history into the War of the Roses when you stumble into a university history department somewhere on the Internet. (This overchoice of informational resources is called "Future Shock," a term coined by writer Alvin Toffler several years back.)

8. Keeping in mind the importance of disciplined and focused research, you should also maintain a continual willingness to scrap your initial Internet research findings and use different keywords or take a look at Web, Gopher, and FTP sites other than those you using if they aren't yielding good results. Let's say for example you are looking for cultural information on gay events, happenings, and writings: Do you use the word "gay" or "homosexual" as a key word? If you use just the word "homosexual," you are likely to run across information of a more scientific nature, pertaining to human sexuality. If the information you are finding is a "red herring," then go back and start again. In this example, adding "lifestyle, "culture," or "books" to the keyword search might yield better results. Also, if you have passed by a home page that seemed more relevant to your research, use the "back" arrow function that all Web browsers have to go back and look at that page.

9. What happens when you can't find the answer to your question? Look at your resources. Are they appropriate to your search needs? For example: Are you trying to search for a piece of legislation the contains the word "communications"? If you use any of the larger search engines for this keyword you will get thousands more "hits" than you want. Instead, go to a specific Internet resource related to the subject (i.e. "legislation") such as THOMAS at the Library of Congress. In general, as you begin your research, try to find the particular resource related to your query. In a traditional library, you wouldn't use a periodical guide to look for books. Using the right resource holds true on and off the Net.

10. How do you know when you have successfully concluded your research on the Internet? This can be problematic in part because of the large scale of information on some Internet topics, which precludes looking through it all. But often you can tell your search is over for the simple reason that you have answered the information question that you first posed: What are the opening lines of the Gettysburg Address? What year did Columbus discover America? What did the Supreme Court decide regarding abortion in *Roe v. Wade*? In Internet research, as in other mediums, the question of concluding your research is often inherent in the question you posed to begin with.

Some On-line Guides to the Internet

■ A Little about YAHOO

Using a subject-oriented directory such as YAHOO, which has links to more than 100,000 different Web sites, is an excellent way to begin any "topical" search of the Internet. Started by two Stanford University students who began compiling URLs one day, YAHOO stands for "Yet Another Hierarchical Officious Oracle" and has become known as the most well-organized guide to the Net.

YAHOO now also employs an actual librarian, Srinija Srinivasan, who catalogs and classifies each Web page that is submitted to YAHOO. The classification system used is intended to be as intuitive as a card catalog. Using a modified Dewey decimal system, the subject directory is broken into basic categories such as Arts, Business and Economy, Government, Social Science, Health, and the like. This service also provides free access to the Reuters newswire. As a testament of its usefulness, over 1.5 million visitors-a-week drop into this Web site to avail themselves of its well-indexed informational categories.

YAHOO was previously hosted by the Internet server at Stanford University, and then joined the private sector after its creators—former graduate students David Filo and Jerry Yang—attracted some investment funds. The site is still free, like everything else on the Net, but there are now low-key "commercials" on the site. The YAHOO Directory address is:

http://www.yahoo.com

■ The Internet Resource Clearinghouse at the University of Michigan

While perhaps not as popular among the average Internet researcher as YAHOO, the Internet guide hosted by The University of Michigan School of Information and Library Studies is arguably one of the top spots for beginning your information hunting. Known as "the Clearinghouse for Subject-Oriented Internet Resource Guides," this Internet locale has links to vast information, organized and cross-referenced under literally hundreds of topics.

This guidepost for information can be reached through the World Wide Web (using a URL), through Gopherspace, or using FTP:

- For Web access, go to http://http2.sils.umich.edu
- Using FTP, travel to una.hh.lilb.umich.edu
- And in Gopherspace, go to gopher.lib.umich.edu

Finding Expert Sources

ProfNet is the answer to an information professional's dream. It's an on-line resource which swiftly provides the names and phone numbers of top experts on almost any subject. Started just two years ago by Dan Forbush, a public information officer at a college in New York, ProfNet grew swiftly and now includes sources at 730 colleges, universities, and a wide range of government, corporate, and nonprofit organizations oriented to scholarship and research.

All the top universities, medical schools, and business schools are members, as are foreign colleges, federal government entities such as the National Science Foundation and the National Institutes of Health, and corporate research labs run by AT&T and IBM.

The concept is brilliant in its simplicity and in the way it swiftly responds to the needs of researchers.

A reporter, for example, is working on a story about widgets. He contacts ProfNet (by e-mail, fax, or telephone) and briefly describes his story and his need for sources. ProfNet sends the query to its network of some 1,500 public information officers at 730 participating institutions.

Each query is sent to all the participating institutions. It's up to the public information officer (PIO) at the college to monitor the queries and respond if his institution has the kind of expert being sought.

In short order, the reporter who submitted the query gets responses by e-mail, fax, or telephone from PIOs who provide the names, brief biographies, addresses, and phone numbers of widget experts at their institutions.

Then it is up to the researcher to contact the source for an interview.

Most journalists love it. "I think it's incredible that there's one place where I can send a query and within twenty-four hours have public information officers from around the world responding," says Leah Ingram, a magazine writer.

"ProfNet really shines, even when I only give them a day to find me an expert on something difficult and obscure," adds *Voice of America* reporter and anchor Jim Randle.

"It may be the single most useful thing on the Net for the working Internaut," says Neil Reisner, database editor at the *Bergen Record*. "We have used ProfNet to gather sources for a major project on juvenile justice, for stories on home education, educational finance, on health and parenting issues, and countless others."

ProfNet's creator Forbush says the on-line service handles 150 to 200 queries in a typical week. About half of them are from newspaper and wire service reporters, about one-fourth are from radio and television reporters, and about one-fourth are from magazine writers.

There are no barriers to the Internaut who wants to access ProfNet. Forbush says he occasionally must check out questioners to make sure they are legitimate members of the press, and not individuals doing non-journalistic research.

The institutions who are members of ProfNet are anxious to cooperate with reporters and editors in the hope that this will result in stories that cast a favorable light on their organizations. For that reason, there's no fee charged reporters who query ProfNet.

You may deliver queries to ProfNet as follows:

- By Internet: http://www.vyne.com/profnet
- By e-mail to: profnet@vyne.com
- By fax: 516-689-1425
- By phone: 1-800-PROFNET or 516-941-3736

If you have questions or need assistance, call Dan Forbush, the ProfNet sysop, or Kevin Aschenbrenner, ProfNet distribution chief, at 1-800-PROFNET.

Internet Information Hunting: Case Studies

The following stories and examples will help you understand how to approach and do research on the Internet. In these case studies we look at everything from a veteran journalist and academic researcher, Christopher Simpson, and how he brings an inquiring mind to bear on the Net, to looking at how a public relations specialist at the prestigious National Institutes of Health is grappling with the task of making large volumes of information available via the Net.

These case studies are intended to help you develop a mindset for conducting useful research on the Internet by introducing real situations like those you will encounter in your own research. Through these examples, you will also begin to develop an anecdotal understanding of how information is ordered on the Net. Remember, the Internet is not a library. There is no catalog and no single way to find what you're looking for. Among the first resources an Internet researcher needs are a sense of the kinds of resources they are likely to find, and what the best means of finding them might be.

Looking for Law and Justice Throughout the Web

For professor Christopher Simpson, the Internet is a research tool of vast potential but using it effectively is dependent on the knowledge of the real world and on the traditional research skills and expertise that a researcher brings to it.

Simpson, a communications professor at The American University in Washington, D.C., frequently teaches the effective use of the

71

Internet. In his latest such class, his students produced a guidebook to law and justice resources that can be found on the Net.

"I think it's a very effective and powerful research tool, whose full power has yet to be realized," Simpson said. His warnings about it included that it is still "more complicated than it need be," and also that some resources require some patience to access because they "clog up with users."

But all things considered, Simpson said that for many types of research jobs, the Internet is far quicker; particularly for going through library card catalogs from one's desktop. "If the Net is useful for anything, it's that it permits people to do some existing jobs better," said Simpson of how Internet research is an enhancement and not a substitute for of good research skills.

The research skills that Simpson brings to the Internet are the skills that he teaches to his students—those of the hard-nosed journalist who follows up on initial information with even more questions. Having an inquisitive mind naturally leads one to more information, he emphasized. "What you do with information comes back to individual initiatives."

He tells the story of how, using the vast Lexis/Nexus database (which isn't on the Net), some of his students found a story of how a man died suspiciously during his arrest for drunk and disorderly conduct. Facts in the story made the students question the role of police chokeholds during such an arrest.

Using key words from this first story, the students went to the Internet to develop background information.

"They found material suggestive of a pattern," said Simpson of how the larger story focused increasingly on the use of chokeholds by police. Further research using the Net and other sources included looking into police training practices involving the chokehold.

"Are police trained when to use and not to use the chokehold?" he asked. "The advantage of using the Internet is that you can do much of this research in forty-five minutes from your desktop computer."

This speed of research, however, is dependent on whether the information you are looking for accessible via the Internet or not, Simpson cautions. If something hasn't been put on the Net yet—then, of course, it is inaccessible via the Net. But, even if certain resources aren't actually on the Net, often a researcher will a least come across a reference to a certain resource or author that they might not have known about that can be looked further into at a library.

For reporters and other types of researchers, the Internet is a way to keep one's finger on the pulse of their "beat" or interest area, Simpson added. This is particularly true of keeping posted on subjects from Internet newsgroups and by using ProfNet (described above). Harking back to the research of law and justice topics, Simpson cites that police officers are some of the most enthusiastic users of computer bulletin boards and newsgroups, and that these are good places to get in touch with them to gain information.

"The Internet can leverage a reporter's time," Simpson said. He also pointed out how many police departments are starting to use Internet resources such as Web pages to increase departmental interaction with the community and that keeping track of these community, liaison efforts can in turn generate new story material.

Simpson recommends some of the following Internet locales for looking into topics of law and justice:

- U.S. Department of Justice
  http://www.usdoj.gov

- Dr. Cecil Greek's Criminal Justice Page
  http://www.stpt.usf.edu/~greek/cj.html

- Police Resource List
  http://police.sas.ab.ca/prl/index.html

- U.S. Supreme Court Decisions
  http://www.law.cornell.edu/supct/

- American Bar Association
  http://www.abanet.org

73

Intuitive Garden Research

The following first-person account shows a researcher using the Internet more intuitively than is often possible with conventional research tools. It's very easy to just keep looking around until you find what you're looking for. This case study focuses on how a writer, Carlene Smart, uses the Internet to help her write about gardening.

Plant Bulbs vs. Light Bulbs: Researching Gardening
by Carlene Smart

"You can, with the switch of a button or two, have your plants planted, gown, arranged, and groomed—without weeds," said Sue Rogers in Jonquiere, Québec.

"I make gardens, I make more gardens; my husband has to drag me away from my computer to go teach my classes. It helped me do a lot to determine things I can't do when buying seedlings—like which textures of foliage will combine well," said Carol Wallace of Clarks Summit, Pennsylvania.

They are talking about a gardening software program called A Garden in Time. I found out about it while researching new products for "computer gardeners."

The Internet is the perfect place for gardeners to spend their winter months. With the wealth of information available through universities, government, and research programs, facts and figure are at your fingertips. The Internet is a storehouse of information available for everyday people.

When I received a writing assignment on "The Glory of Bulbs," I went to the Net. Using Netscape, a World Wide Web browser, I clicked the button for Internet Search and was given my choice of search engines. I chose several over the next five minutes, including one at Carnegie Mellon University, and one that would search the Usenet. When I typed in the word "bulbs," I discovered I had to narrow the search. I got everything from "light bulbs" to "light bulb jokes."

Then I typed in "flowers, bulbs" and was off in the right direction. Not only did I get my information, I found several new products to include in the article I was writing, and I purchased several for my own garden. When a neighbor had problems with her roses, I again connected to the Internet and searched through several different sections of the Internet directory YAHOO. In YAHOO I chose the "Home and Garden" menu, then went into "FAQ—The Rose" to see the answers to frequently asked questions about roses and found what I needed.

When I needed to know how to prune my apple tree, I went to YAHOO again, and in "Home and Garden" I chose the "Tree Doctor." While this may sound circular, to find what you are looking for on the Internet, you just have keep trying different places until you find what you are searching for. I needed to find out what was available for gardening software, and found out about A Garden In Time. Also I found out about the "Bulb Bopper," a new tool for planting flower bulbs. It hooks onto a drill, and after you insert the bulbs, you measure the depth and Bulb Bopper does the work for you.

When I find a file that I can use on the Net, I click on the file, save, and in seconds it's on my hard drive. I also recommend that when you find of source of information that you like on the Net, you bookmark the location on your browser so you can zip back there anytime.

Internet newsgroups are a good way to pass away the frosty nights and still keep your hand in at gardening. There are more than 20,000 such groups—each dealing with a particular affinity—with groups that gardeners would enjoy including rec.gardens, rec.food, and misc.rural.

The abbreviation before the word tells you what kind of newsgroup it is—"rec" is recreations, "sci" is the prefix for a science group, and "misc" is for a miscellaneous group. Once you have accessed a newsgroup you can read what others have said or join in with your own comments. But be sure and read the FAQ section that is usually available for each group.

No matter what your level of expertise in gardening, you will learn a lot in a short time. Along with having access to so much varied information, you can meet like-minded people and share information around the world.

Here's where to find some of the garden spots on the Internet:

- Garden Web Directory
        http://www.btw.com

- The Garden Encyclopedia
  http://www.btw.com/garden-archive/toc.html

- Bulb Bopper
  http://www.tyrell.net

Hunting for the Perfect Cup of Coffee on the Internet

For some reason, coffee and computers just seem to go together. Therefore it seems natural that coffeehouses and computers should also go together. The following story is an example of how you might first hear about a certain home page or newsgroup while traveling in the off-line (real) world. It helps, of course, to travel with an inquiring mind and a notebook to jot down URLs.

Specifically, I (T. K. Maloy) happened onto what is known as a "cybercafe" in Dublin, Ireland and discovered a list on the Internet of cybercafes around the world.

Teenage German girls surrounded the computer terminal—fascinated, pulled in—as they read *Die Welt*, the daily newspaper of Hamburg. But they weren't in Hamburg, or anywhere near Germany for that matter. They were tourists in Ireland, and, like me, they had managed to stumble upon the recently opened Underground Club, a cybersalon and cognitive coffee shop, as it were.

Pat Woods is proprietor of the Underground, one of several cybercafes in Dublin. He is a believer in what science fiction author William Gibson called "The Matrix," an electronic, synthetic world that is woven of vast computer networks. It is Gibson who coined the now-famous term *cyberspace* to describe the alternative reality created by The Matrix.

His Underground Club is just one of hundreds these new types of coffee shops worldwide, that are offer not only coffee but a gateway to the brave new world of the World Wide Web.

I found, while I was at the club, that Mark Dziecielewski, a United Kingdom resident, had compiled a Word Wide Web home page listing these institutions and with hyperlinks to many of them (http://www.easynet.co.uk/pages/cafe/ccafe.htm). His Cyber Cafe Guide listed over 110 cafes boasting Internet access with their coffee service.

The guide listed many cybercafes in the United States: from the ICON Byte Bar & Grill in San Francisco and the Internet Cafe in Scranton, Pennsylvania, to The Hard Drive Cafe in Wichita, Kansas. Standing in the Underground in Dublin, I was able to read what the Bean Central cybercafe in Nashville, Tennesee, has to say about itself:

> Bean Central opened in April 1986 as a specialty coffee roaster and coffee bar. Now in April 1995, we have expanded with a comfortable 35-seat cafe. We have two Pentiums 75s w16 meg running wfwg 3.11 and Mosaic through a router, up an ISDN line to our provider and the WWW. We will add more machines as demand increases and if the Webbers are not too rowdy.

These cybercafes certainly seem to be proliferating and offer something of a service to interested Net novices and veterans alike. Some even bill themselves as available to traveling business types who may just need a power point to use their laptops. Like the ubiquitous Kinko's that acts as the "branch office" for businesses which have no desktop publishing capability, the cybercafes may become the Internet access point for myriads of people. At these cognitive coffee shops of the future one won't need to own of expensive computer equipment to get wired.

If there isn't a coffee shop with Internet access in your locality now, there is liable to be one coming soon.

Other Coffee-Related Internet Resources:

- alt.drugs.caffeine (coffee and serious caffeine abuse)
- alt.coffee
- alt.food.coffee
- rec.food.drink.coffee

Evaluating Information

The following is a case study in judging the veracity of some information that you will come across on the Internet. There is a category of information that became known as "urban legends" some years ago (i.e. "the cat in the microwave," etc.); and these perennial legends, and many new ones, have found their way onto the Internet, where they have gone into overdrive.

A recent example (winter 1996) is a story that has been actively circulating on Internet newsgroups and through chain e-mail about astronaut Neil Armstrong cryptically saying "Good luck, Mr. Gorsky" when he set foot on the moon. To see what this is all about, read on.

What Did Neil Armstrong Really Say on the Moon?

From corporate offices to scientific research labs there has been e-mail received—passed on by friends and such—which contains the account of a speech by astronaut Neil Armstrong to a group in Tampa Bay, Florida.

According to the account, Armstrong was asked about why he said "Good luck, Mr. Gorsky" during his moon mission. The account cites the fact that Armstrong has been asked this question before, but always declined to answer it. This time, however, he at last came forward with an explanation.

Armstrong said that at long last he could freely answer this question because the Mr. Gorsky in question was dead. It seems that as a boy, Armstrong's family lived next to a family named Gorsky. One day while playing ball with his brother in the backyard, Armstrong found himself chasing a pop fly into the neighbor's backyard, where it landed right outside the Gorskys's bedroom window.

According to the story, young Armstrong hears raised voices as he is retrieving the ball and he pauses to listen and overhears Mrs. Gorsky shrieking at her husband, "Oral sex? Oral sex you want. You'll get oral sex when the kid next door walks on the moon!"

And the rest is history. Or is it?

According to NASA spokesman Brian Welch, a review of transcripts from Armstrong's Apollo 11 mission contains no reference of any kind to "Mr. Gorsky." Other knowledgeable sources also dispute the truth of this story.

But because of the global dissemination of this tale via the Internet, it is dependably passed around as truth with little to stop it in lieu of someone sending mass e-mail unmasking the story as erroneous. Also, because the Internet passes material along in print, as opposed to stories passed around at the office water cooler, the stories have the credibility often attributed to printed matter.

"With the Internet, there's an enormous amount of information that hasn't been filtered through anything. It didn't have to find a publisher, it didn't have to go through peer review to become available to an enormous amount of people," said a scientist familiar with the Net in a recent news interview.

"Good luck, Mr. Gorsky" has become what's known as a "Netmyth." And because these Netmyths can be massively duplicated word-for-word via e-mail and other means, this begs the question of how to judge information.

One good rule of thumb is the old "consider the source" rule. While there is much "unfiltered" information on the Net that hasn't been vetted by news organizations or scholarly journals as being accurate, the majority of the information available via the Net is from credible sources.

If you read information straight from the NASA Web site (http://www.nasa.gov), for instance, you can safely say that that material carries with it the credibility of that organization. Here, for instance, is part of a strange-but-true press release from NASA about a "space disturbance" detected in the fall of 1995, from NASA'S Goddard Space Flight Center at ftp://pao.gsfc.nasa.gov/pub/PAO/releases/1995/95-202.txt:

SPACE DISTURBANCE DETECTED BY NASA SATELLITE
BEFORE REACHING EARTH

A NASA spacecraft detected a huge interplanetary disturbance which struck the Earth's protective magnetic field on October 18, producing a magnetic storm and auroral displays, or "Northern Lights" that persisted for two days.

The phenomenon was visible in the United States as far south as Denver, according to scientists at NASA's Goddard Space Flight Center, Greenbelt, MD, who reported critical satellite data to other government agencies and scientists around the world.

The credibility that you grant NASA stands true of government Web sites as well. The myriad well-known newspapers and magazines now publishing on the Internet carry with them their own credibility. And official university sites can be relied upon for research and other scholarly information that they have.

But in this same vein, you must watch out for what you may find through a university student's personal Web page, as scholarly as it may seem. You must bring the skepticism you would normally bring to propaganda when looking through the home pages of political candidates or parties. And researchers must particularly be on guard when looking at the Internet material of fringe groups or of other organizations with an ax to grind.

What's on the Net?

The following is an example of how people within an organization (in this instance, the National Institute of Health) go about making information available through the Internet. This is illustrative of what a big project it is, putting all the world's information out on the Net; and also illustrates the fact that not everything is available yet, but is on its way to being there.

We open with an excerpt from a report about the need for putting health information onto the Internet.

WHAT IS THE ROLE OF INFORMATION IN POPULATION-BASED PUBLIC HEALTH?

MAKING A HEALTHY ON-LINE CONNECTION: THE NATIONAL INSTITUTES OF HEALTH AND ITS NET EFFORTS

The extent to which public health achieves its mission depends, in large part, on the availability of accurate, comparable, timely, and complete information. In fact, one could say that the collection, analysis, use, and communication of health-related information is the quintessential public health service, undergirding all others. The three types of information needs outlined below cut across all of the essential services of public health. Meeting these needs depends not only on a supportive technical infrastructure, but also on personnel with the skills to use emerging technologies (both to communicate and to translate complex data into meaningful information), and on a willingness among professionals in different sectors to work together toward common goals. [From: The Health of the Public and the National Information Infrastructure. Found at: gopher://gopher.nlm.nih.gov/00/nlminfo/ newsletters/reports/niiph.txt]

Mary Jane Walker, a media relations official at the National Institutes of Health, has the Internet on her mind lately and as part of her job description.

She is responsible for starting to guide the National Institute of Allergy and Infectious Diseases (NIAID—one of the seventeen different Institutes at NIH) onto the Net in order to help make vast amounts of research information and breaking health news available to the public and to the press. Already, she points out, NIH has some large-scale on-line and Internet resources such as the National Library of Medicine, but her mandate is to get the NIAID more squarely onto the Information Highway.

"Traditionally we have done everything using mailing lists," says Walker in reference to the actual mailing of hundreds of thousands of press releases and media advisories over the years. But this ongoing effort is, of course, expensive, and she said that some of the media inevitably complained that they were getting press materials too late: "Some press would call and say that they got scooped."

From the NIAID side of the fence, there was also the problem that probably reams and reams of press releases were not reaching the right reporter or going to organization where they were unwanted, thus further wasting money.

"If we are lucky enough, we get to the health reporter that we want and we get some coverage," Walker says.

To cut down on this mass mailing and to further target information releases, Walker says that her office first started reaching a core group of health reporters through the use of faxes.

"We began batch-faxing through the computer," she says.

These various means to reach the press and public with information are what Walker terms her office's "proactive efforts." On the "reactive" side is the answering of the often-frequent phone calls from the press over such hot topics as AIDS/HIV, which adds to the visibility of her office, particularly when new research comes out on this deadly virus.

Now comes the Internet, and the many media and public relations officials at NIH see it as a means to solve both the proactive and reactive problems of spreading information. Walker says that her office already uses e-mail, for instance, to alert some of the media (those with e-mail) of breaking medical news. And she adds that much of NIH is also already "wired" in some fashion or another. But there still much information that is waiting to go on the Net, and Walker and her colleagues are racing to get it there.

"Just this year (1995–1996), the Net began to become a big mandate," Walker says. "We decided how we wanted to reach people and who we wanted to reach."

The result is a NIAID home page, recently gone on-line, that already boasts much information, but has plans for even more dramatic expansion. This page can be found on the World Wide Web at http://www.niaid.nih.gov/

Here you will see a welcoming message, reading:

Welcome to the National Institute of Allergy and Infectious Diseases (NIAID), where scientists work to develop new and improved ways to diagnose, treat, and prevent infectious diseases and disorders of the immune system. Explore NIAID research on AIDS, tuberculosis and other infectious diseases, allergic and immunologic diseases, asthma, transplantation, and more.

Which for the layperson, does help to explain at bit what actually goes on at NIAID.

Once into the page, it includes a link to a NIAID research section and a link to a NIAID Laboratories section, which includes individual links to fourteen different labs such as the Allergic Diseases lab, Immunology lab, and the Infectious Diseases, Molecular Microbiology, Parasitic Diseases, and Viral Diseases labs. The NIAID home page also boast a Newsflash section for press releases.

While working toward getting many more publications onto the Net, Walker notes that many publications and reports are linked to her home page already, such as this "fact sheet" about chronic fatigue syndrome, which begins:

We all get tired; most of us at times have felt depressed. But the enigma known as chronic fatigue syndrome (CFS) is not the ups and downs we experience in everyday life, or even the temporary persistence of such feelings in response to exceptional physical or emotional stress. The early hallmark of the illness is a pronounced fatigue that comes on suddenly and is relentless or relapsing, causing debilitating tiredness or easy exhaustion in someone who has no apparent reason for feeling this way. Unlike the mind fog of a serious hangover, to which CFS has been compared, the profound weakness of CFS does not go away with a few good nights of sleep but instead slyly steals a person's vigor over months and sometimes years. [Found at: http://www.niaid.gov/factsheets/cfs.htm]

Here is an even more dire fact sheet about the initial discovery of AIDS and the course of the epidemic since then.

AIDS—acquired immune deficiency syndrome—was first reported in the United States in 1981 and has since become a major worldwide epidemic. AIDS is caused by the human immunodeficiency virus (HIV). By killing or impairing cells of the immune system, HIV progressively destroys the body's ability to fight infections and certain cancers. Individuals diagnosed with AIDS are susceptible to life-threatening diseases called opportunistic infections, which are caused by microbes that usually do not cause illness in healthy people.

More than 400,000 cases of AIDS have been reported in the United States since 1981, and an estimated 1 million Americans are believed to be infected with HIV. This fact sheet summarizes what is currently known about HIV infection. [Found at: http://www.niaid.nih.gov/factsheets/hivinf.htm]

Walker plans to put even more material up within the near future, including several regularly published newsletters, and to make the large-scale internal database of research reports not only available, but also easily searchable, by experts and the public. She also noted that using the Net as a publishing and distribution medium not only cuts down on mailing costs, but also makes NIH information more easily available on a national and international scale.

Those interested in researching through the various Internet resources at NIAID should note that it has an excellent Gopher archive that has been in place for several years, and includes not only material from the Institute of Allergies and Infectious Diseases, but also has a search function for staff telephone numbers throughout the NIH and a link to all the Gopher servers at NIH.

The Gopher address at the NIAID is gopher://gopher.niaid.nih.gov/

The NIAID is just one of seventeen different institutes that come under the authority of the National Institutes of Health. A partial list of other NIH institutes includes: the National Cancer Institute, National Eye Institute, National Institute on Aging, National Institute on Alcohol Abuse and Alcoholism, National Institute of Drug Abuse, and the National Institute of Mental Health.

One can link to all these various institutes from the NIH home page of Institutes and Offices at http://www.nih.gov/icd/

The National Library of Medicine, located at the U.S. National Institutes of Health (NIH) in Bethesda, Maryland, is the world's largest library dealing with a single scientific/professional topic. It cares for over 4.5 million holdings (including books, journals, reports, manuscripts, and audio-visual items). The NLM offers extensive on-line information services (dealing with clinical care, toxicology and environmental health, and basic biomedical research), has several active research and development components (including an extramural grants program), houses an extensive history of medicine collection, and provides several programs designed to improve the nation's medical library system.

The opening page for the library is at http://www.nlm.nih.gov/

For a full rundown of the all the available on-line resources at the National Library of Medicine, go to this URL: http://www.nlm.nih.gov/top_level.dir/nlm_online_info.html

Included in the listing here are such well-regarded, searchable databases as MEDLARS, TOXNET, and Grateful Med, which is a more user-friendly interface into MEDLARS. One caveat: all these databases require user accounts and access codes, so they aren't for the casual researcher. But for anyone in the business of researching medical information, for whatever reason, these resources are indispensable.

Citing Sources: Footnotes for the Electronic Age

Perhaps the most serious responsibility of doing research is crediting those ideas which are not one's own. Students and journalists alike are constantly reminded of the consequences of not properly crediting one's own research, and several style manuals exist to help scholars record their citations uniformly and accurately. This responsibility can be characterized in the form of the Chinese proverb that asks, "If a tree falls in the forest and no one is there to hear it, does it make any sound?" Similarly, if a journalist or scholar can't physically produce their research, how does one know it ever existed?

The wealth of electronic information has posed the twofold problem of how to cite the information and how to retrieve the information later when Internet addresses and Web sites are constantly changing. Most traditional citation formats include the title, author, publication, and date, as well as page number. This information allows future researchers to go back and retrieve and/or verify the citation. With electronic information, however, page numbers are almost non-existent. Publication dates (in the form of time/date stamps on a home page) are more common, but with the constant weeding and updating of Web information, what is accessed today may be gone tomorrow.

The standard style guides, including Turabian and MLA (Modern Language Association), have taken a stab at creating standards for citing electronic resources, and a few scholars have published their own style guides on the Internet. All of these style guides vary in their treatment of electronic information. Turabian's guide, for example, includes the date the information was accessed on the Internet, while Janice Walker's guide includes the date published on the Internet.

As always, the best strategy in citing sources is to pick one method and be consistent. If there is a specific method already being used by your colleagues, use that method. Another tip is to print a copy of the research you gather from the Internet with a time/date stamp, which can be used later if you need it.

Here is a bibliography of relevant citation resources that can be found in print or on the Internet:

Li, Xia and Crane, Nancy. *The Official Internet World Guide to Electronic Styles: A Handbook to Citing Electronic Information.* Westport: Meckler Media, 1996.

Examples from their book can be found at the following Internet address: http://www.rpi.edu/dept/chem/cheminfo/cistudio/module4/elcite.html

Gibaldi, Joseph. *MLA Handbook for Writers of Research Papers.* New York: Modern Language Association of America, 1995.

Turabian, Kate L. *A Manual for Writers of Term Papers, Theses, and Dissertations.* Chicago: University of Chicago Press, 1996.

Walker, Janice. *MLA-Style Citations of Electronic Sources.* Published on the World Wide Web at http://www.casusf.edu/english/walker/mla.html

■

CHAPTER 6

Internet Sleuthing with Search Engines

by Suzanne Kincheloe

Anyone can "surf" through home pages or "lurk" on a Listserv and discover good resources. But this method of searching is fairly time-consuming and only occasionally reliable. That's why Internet users of all abilities flock to Internet search engines to perform that panacea of information-gathering—the keyword search.

The concept of "searching," plunking in keywords and having a system respond with hits, is common to anyone who has used a commercial on-line service or a library's on-line catalog. Internet search engines look and act a lot like typical databases. Instead of an archive or catalog of records, though, they search a collection of Web resources, Usenet news, or some other section of the Internet. Computer programs called spiders, robots, or worms randomly visit and collect data about sites on the Internet. The data, usually an abstracted version of the home page, is compiled in a "catalog," which is searched by the user.

Search engines may look and act like the databases many of us find indispensable at work and school, but the standard cautions for any kind of on-line searching apply even more so on the Internet. The sheer amount of information available on the Internet makes it very likely that a search will get something, anything, in return. An avid public library user, for example, who is used to getting twenty hits at his local system, may think he is onto something big when Lycos returns three hundred Web sites. But the question is, are the sites useful? If not, is there a strategy that could greatly improve his results?

Many Internet searchers are happy if they find what they need in the first ten or twenty hits. Some researchers, however, need more conclusive answers. In those situations, the searcher needs to be armed with knowledge of search options, subject directories, and some characteristics of the search engine itself. While Internet searching is inherently an organic process, this chapter will sketch out some guiding principles for getting the most out of these resources.

Basic Search Skills: Completing the Search Form

Internet search engines vary greatly in the size and types of databases, but there are some basic features common to all of them. Once you have accessed a search site on the World Wide Web, the first thing you will see is a search form with a keyword blank, a "Search" button, and an "Options" button. To perform a search, simply enter your keywords and click on the Search key. These simple search forms seem to work the best when the searcher knows exactly what he or she needs. For example, the title of a home page or the name of a person or company tend to get the best results. In the absence of an exact name or title, a combination of a broad term with a narrower term (e.g. "business, Pacific Rim"), will also get good results from a simplified search form.

Many people prefer this "keyword and go" method of searching, but it does not always get the best results. If you retrieve copious results or find several "false hits," containing the keywords but not the content, you may need to click on the "Options" button. The next screen will offer another search form, with a keyword blank and more settings. If you've never used a particular search engine before, read the documentation or reference this book to guide you in selecting the right settings.

Beyond Boolean: Fuzzy Logic and Other Features

Those who are familiar with on-line searching know the traditional Boolean connectors: "and," "or," "not." With these three simple terms, one can connect broad and narrow concepts to retrieve a nice, neat package or set of resources from a database. Internet search engines operate differently on this score, although the concepts of "and," "or," "not," are generally the same. Consider this extended example:

A school librarian in Florida is looking for hurricane resources for a science unit on natural disasters. She hopes to put the resources up on the school's home page for the students to use in their projects. Since she's looking for resources on the 1995 hurricane season, she writes these keywords on a piece of paper:

Marilyn Luis Opal hurricane

Then she clicks on the "Options" button of her search engine, to see what connectors she can choose. Most search engines offer at least two choices: Any or All. If she chooses "Any," the search engine will possibly return documents containing just "Marilyn," or on hurricanes in general. If she chooses "All," the search engine will return only those documents that mention all the terms, "Marilyn," "Luis," "Opal," and "hurricane."

Depending on the search engine, she can choose from several other search features that will mimic Boolean searching. On Lycos, for example, she can match two or three terms, thus getting results that would approximate the Boolean statement above. Lycos will also find variations of words, such as plurals or different tenses. The default is a "loose" match, which will pick up the most variations of a word. The best option for the above example is a "strong" match, because the searcher knows exactly what she wants, and does not want any pages about opals authored by Marilyn Jones. This type of search feature is called "fuzzy logic," because it uses guidelines, like number of terms and various strengths of matching, to get the result.

OpenText, on the other hand, offers a "Power Search" feature, which will allow our searcher to enter each keyword in a separate blank, and choose a specific connector to operate between each keyword. For each keyword, she can also select where she wants the word to be in the home page. Thus, she can search for Any Marilyn, Any Opal, Any Luis, with "hurricane" in the title.

Enhanced Services

Ever since Lycos and YAHOO moved from "educational" servers to "commercial" servers, the searching software business has grown more competitive. Now, searching the Web has become necessary for the most basic of interests, and software is scrambling to have the friendliest interfaces and access to the most Web sites and newsgroups. But as these databases catalog millions of Web pages, so the search results can become more redundant and cumbersome.

The upshot of this competition has resulted in research sites that allow the user to browse by subject as well as search by keyword. Subject directories are compiled by human editors and arranged hierarchically for browsing. Subject directories are a good place to find quick answers to general questions. On the other hand, a keyword search tends to get the best results when you need to locate a specific resource or mass a broad collection of URLs. Almost all search engines now offer a variety of methods for getting at information. YAHOO, for example, offers a keyword search of its indices, while Lycos, which started out as a robot search engine, now features a hand-compiled directory.

Below is a listing, in no particular order, of search engines that have grown from slow-ticking robots and hand-compiled indices to leaders in this new industry. The discussion of them is by no means an endorsement of the products, but merely an illustration of where Internet searching is headed.

■ Lycos

http://www.lycos.com

- *Database Construction:* Automated and by submission of URLs
- *Fields Indexed:* URL, URL references, title, headings, 20 lines of text, 100 weighty words
- *Update Frequency:* Weekly
- *Number of Pages:* Over 10 million, or 91 percent of the Web
- *Browsable Subject Directory:* Yes

- *Search Options:* Lycos underwent a major revamping in October of 1995, and now offers a simple "keyword and go" search blank. As mentioned in the Boolean Searching section, "fuzzy" search options are available. One option will match any two to seven words in the search string. Another will find variations of words, from a "loose match," which yields the most hits, to a "strong match," which will only pull up the exact words in the string.

- *Note:* Lycos indexes not only home pages on the Web, but also the individual links within each home page. This process enables Lycos to rank pages by their popularity. It will, however, produce several hits that are exactly the same, which can make for an onerous amount of redundant hits. Some searchers choose to use this idiosyncrasy to select which sites they want to visit, although Lycos does offer reviews with each site they index. Other searchers, however, may weary of the redundancy and seek out another service.

  Lycos also has links to the most popular Web sites, as well as to current news. You may also subscribe to a service that will keep you up to date on current Web sites of interest to you.

■ OpenText

http://www.opentext.com

- *Database Construction:* Automated, and by submission of URLs
- *Fields Indexed:* URL, URL references, full text
- *Update Frequency:* Weekly
- *Browsable Subject Directory:* No
- *Search Options:* This enhanced search engine offers three types of searching—simple, power, or weighted—for a greater variety of options and results. A simple search will retrieve basic keywords or entire phrases, and resembles the "blank" search forms of other services. OpenText also provides a service called "WebPulse," which lists the top fifty accessed Web sites each day.

  If you do not get the results you want from a simple search, try a power search. This allows your to search by URL, title, or summary information. The power search will also allow you to attach connectors to individual keywords, so you can perform Boolean searching with multiple connectors.

Perhaps the most notable feature of OpenText is that after every search it offers an opportunity to improve your search, and then offers a suggestion on how to do this. For example, when our librarian received two hits for landlocked territories like Alberta, Canada, she decided to try to improve her results. OpenText gave this librarian an extra keyword blank, and only offered the "presence/absence" option to her weighted search.

- *Note:* Users of OpenText may register with the service, entitling them to on-line support. OpenText is also a software company, which sells its hypertext searching software to organizations with large internal networks, also known as "intranets."

■ YAHOO

http://www.yahoo.com

- *Database Construction:* Manual, and by submission of URLs
- *Fields Indexed:* URL, title, comments
- *Update Frequency:* Daily
- *Browsable Subject Directory:* Yes
- *Search Options:* YAHOO offers Boolean searching, and will let you choose whether to search for complete words or substrings, or variations on the keyword. The default on YAHOO is "and" and substrings. To change these default settings, go to the "Search Options" screen.
- *Note:* YAHOO was one of the first services to take the principle of editing Web sites seriously. The site offers jumping-off points for surfing the Web, including a list of "What's Cool," "What's New," and even a "Random Link." YAHOO is a complete subject index that anticipates your keywords and offers general information for those quick-reference questions. The "Recreation" and "Drugs" headings will get a quick listing of the DEA's list of controlled substances, as well information on the War on Drugs and a list of "Natural Highs." From the "Reference" section, one can check the CIA World Fact Book and basic etiquette questions.

■ Excite

http://www.excite.com

- *Database Construction:* Automated, and by submission of URLs
- *Number of Pages:* over 1.5 million
- *Browsable Subject Directory:* Yes
- *Search Options:* To perform a search, simply enter your keywords (Excite gives you a choice between "keywords" or "words describing a concept," but I've found no significant difference in the search results), choose what form you want (Web, Usenet, or both), and send it off.

  Like Lycos, Excite will rank each hit by its probability of relevance. Excite, however, has a feature called "interactive browsing" which allows a user to make links from one good hit to another page like it. OpenText offers a similar feature. This can help in those situations where you know there's more information than what is on your "hit list."
- *Note:* Excite provides headline news, an index of over 35,000 reviews of Web sites, and classified ads.

■ Alta-Vista

http://www.altavista.digital.com/

- *Database Construction:* Automated, and by submission of URLs
- *Fields Indexed:* URL, URL references, title, headings, 20 lines of text, 100 weighty words
- *Update Frequency:* Weekly
- *Number of Pages:* 22 million
- *Browsable Subject Directory:* Yes
- *Search Options:* Alta Vista searches the Web and the Usenet, and of the many search engines, this one appears to make the best use of Boolean search features.

  In the "Simple Query" form, you should put quotation marks around keywords that you want to appear next to each other in your search. In "Advanced query," you should write the Boolean connectors into the search string.

  This engine comes with complete instructional documen-tation which will give you tips on such things as searching for phrases, using parentheses, and using dates to limit the scope of your search and the volume of your search results.

■ DejaNews

http://www.dejanews.com/

- *Database Construction:* Automated, and by submission of URLs
- *Fields Indexed:* URL, URL references, title, headings, 20 lines of text, 100 weighty words
- *Update Frequency:* Weekly
- *Browsable Subject Directory:* Yes
- *Search Options:* This resource will search Usenet archives and retrieve relevant articles and threads. Search options include pattern matching, filtering, threads, author profiles, and time sensitivity. The basic form asks for keywords, number of hits returned, and a choice of "and" or "or" Boolean logic. The basic search form also features a weighting option, which allows the searcher to change the default to prefer the author, date, or newsgroup. The software allows the user to "create a filter" at the bottom of the form, which will then retrieve articles by author, newsgroup, and date.

■ InfoSeek

http://www.infoseek.com

- *Database Construction:* Manual
- *Fields Indexed:* Title, summary
- *Browsable Subject Directory:* Yes
- *Search Options:* InfoSeek, in addition to providing a simple "keyword and go" search, offers several different options for narrowing your search. First choose the portion of the Internet you want to search, Usenet, FTP, Gopher, or the World Wide Web. Then use the following tags to help narrow your search:
  - ◆ Boolean searching is covered by using (+) before a required word, and a (–) before a negated word.
  - ◆ Put double quotation marks around words that should appear together, i.e., "Pete Wilson."

- ✦ Place a hyphen between words that should appear very close to each other, e.g. AIDS-Hispanic.
- ✦ Use brackets around words that can appear in any order, e.g. [AIDS Hispanic]
- ✦ InfoSeek is case-sensitive, so only capitalize when appropriate.
- ✦ When searching for two unrelated proper names, place a comma between them.

- *Note:* InfoSeek is quick to point out that they are not a search engine, but rather a complete, professional-quality information service. They were the first to charge ($14.95 per month) for its service, but it may be worth the cost. The pay service provides users with access to wire services, periodicals, and a "Personal Newspaper."

■ WebCrawler

http://webcrawler.com

- *Database Construction:* Automated, and by submission of URLs
- *Fields Indexed:* URL, URL references, title, headings, 20 lines of text, 100 weighty words
- *Update Frequency:* Weekly
- *Browsable Subject Directory:* Yes
- *Search Options:* Boolean searching: WebCrawler defaults to searching for "All" of your keywords, but you can uncheck this box to search "Any," of your keywords.
- *Note:* WebCrawler is one of the earliest search engines, and is now featured on America Online. It searches its database of Web documents and titles to match keywords. They offer a listing of the top twenty-five most frequently visited sites on the Web.

■ World Wide Web Worm

http://wwww.cs.colorado.deu/www

or　　　　　　　http://guano.cs.colorado.deu/wwww/

- *Database Construction:* Automated
- *Fields Indexed:* URLS, page titles

- *Browsable Subject Directory:* No
- *Search Options:* The Worm is an early search engine that allowed a search on four different levels of information. This includes all URL eferences (home pages as well as the home pages that cite them), all URL addresses (any home page's address), only in document titles (the most efficient search), or only in document addresses (any document's address). The search engine will match the keywords and build an index of resources.

 Like its contemporaries, the Worm will search for "Any" (meaning "or") or "All" (meaning "and") of your terms.

Meta-Search Engines

One step up from the individual search engine are the meta-search engines. These sites provide a single search blank which is then submitted to several search engines at once. These search engines are good for very comprehensive Internet searching, when one either wants to do the broadest possible search or wants to compare how individual search engines will handle a search. These resources are very powerful, and a few are the preferred choices for many information professionals because they offer so much material on one site.

 The All-in-One search page is one of these rich search sites. It provides search blanks not to specific search engines, but to types of literature and formats of information: Reference Desk, Software, Technical Reports, Publications, News/Weather, and World Wide Web are just a few examples. The search results are listed by type of search engine (all of the DejaNews hits are listed together, for example). The Reference Desk provides access to several criss-cross ZIP code searches, as well as area code searches, 1-800 directories, and even a searchable hacker's glossary (http://www.albany.net/allinone/).

 A service called Savvy Search will submit the keyword blank to one or more search engines, then return the results of those individual search engines. Be sure to refine your search before submitting it to Savvy Search, however, as vague or single-concept searches (e.g. virus) will take a long time to generate results, which in turn may be marginally useful (http://www.cs.colostate.edu/~dreiling/smartform. html).

■

a Directory of Useful and Interesting Web Sites

T he following section of *The Internet Research Guide* covers some of the best Web sites that we have found on the Internet.

Netsurfing is all good and fine—and in fact is one of the best ways to discover new and interesting things—but in the following sections we give you specific Net sites to directly begin your topical research without having to browse around. We have grouped these into twelve basic categories: Culture, Women, Writing, Religion, History, Travel, Government and Politics, International, Business, News, Sports, and Alternative.

That doesn't cover everything, but it's a start. The material provided under each topical area is eclectic and in many ways subjective. And there are not an even amount of URLs listed under each category. But then this eclecticism is in some ways reflective of the Internet itself.

In that same vein, for those of you who are just entering cyberspace: Be advised that it is a dynamic place; things are always changing. By the time some of you open the pages of this book (perhaps years hence) some of these places will have changed their Internet addresses. And some may, for unforeseen reasons, have ceased to exist.

But on the whole, such as with the U.S. government Internet addresses, these sites we have chosen as starting points for your individual research tours into the Internet, will continue to exist for some time. Or if they have changed their locations, they often will have left a "forwarding address" at their old address.

Remember, however, we are a hard copy book about that sometimes ephemeral beast, the Internet, and to keep fully abreast you must go to some of the directory sources and search engines on the Net itself, such as YAHOO directory at http://www.yahoo.com, where you will find more than 100,000 categorized URLs (according to our last count in fall 1995).

That said, Internauts: Happy Hunting!

Culture

This selection of Web sites encompasses cultural activities within the standard scope of mainstream culture, including the fine arts, music, and popular entertainment. In the case of music we will list musical forms from classical to rock-and-roll, which is aged enough at four decades to be considered part of the mainstream.

In our later selection of Alternative sites we will look at newer forms of music—from Punk (now twenty years old, but still somewhat alternative) to Rave—and at other more recent "alternative" additions to the culture of the world.

With regards to the cultural expression of the written word, we have opted to place literary resources in their own section under Writing.

ART ON-LINE A gallery of over 750 women artists from around the world. Inspired by the Fourth World Conference on Women, artist Muriel Magenta uses information technology to create a visual experience in a gallery space and transmit it over the Internet. The World's Women On-Line electronic art network can be found at:

http://www.asu.edu:80/wwol/

THE ART BAR This is the place to find music, food, beer, and wine.

Why? Because art is long and life is short.
http://www.wet.net/wet/artbar

ARTUSA The American Council for the Arts on-line information service.
http://www.artsusa.org.

BEAVIS AND BUTTHEAD "Heh, heh . . . heh, heh, heh heh." This is the page for those two animated youths, who could be the Tom Sawyer and Huck Finn of our day if looked at in the proper light.
http://clavin.hsc.colorado.edu

BIRDLAND'S AUSTRALIAN JAZZ PAGE This page offers jazz and blues reviews, catalogs, bestsellers, album artwork, and selected sounds from Australia and the world.
http://www.magna.com.au/~birdland

BLUES WORLD Provides information, images, and resources about St. Louis and New Orleans blues and jazz music.
http://www.inlink.com/~joelslot

BRADY BUNCH As if this needs an explanation. Let's just say the obvious, that this is all about *The Brady Bunch*, that classic of American television from the seventies. There are also links to other "Brady" pages.
http://www.primenet.com/~dbrady/

BRAZILIAN POPULAR MUSIC Devoted to Brazilian musicians and their works.
http://www.ime.usp.br/~pdjorge/musica/mpb.html

CARTOON WORLD The CW Web site features cool pictures, sound bytes, and a variety of movie clips from old and new favorites on your cartoon list. It ranges from *Teenage Mutant Ninja Turtles* to *Underdog*.
http://www.arias.net/~eriks

DEUTSCHES MUSEUM Here you will find information about exhibitions at the biggest technical museum in Europe. The Deutsches

Museum covers more than 55,00 square meters.

http://www.lrz-mue

DIGITAL AVATAR—SOUTHERN ASIAN ART AND CULTURE This Web site plays host to material from Southern Asia, including art on display and information on culture and religion.

http://www.charm.net/~nayak/avtar2.html

DIGITAL PHOTOGRAPHY 95 The result of a judged competition, with the avowed purpose to "extend the connection between the artist and the viewer," the quality here is above average, compared to some of the other photo compilations found on the Internet. Choose from one of the various walls within the reception area to click on the picture of your choice for a larger image. A click on an artist's name will reveal further information on that individual.

http://www.bradley.edu/exhibits95/

FRIENDS Let's just be *Friends*. Here, one should find everything they want here about the TV show that has taken American by storm and spawned numerous clone shows.

http://www.nbc.com/entertainment/shows/friends/index.hmtl

MILLENNIUM ARTS ONLINE This is a well-designed Cambridge, Massachusetts–based venue that acts as a showcase of the arts, ranging from music, dance, film, and fashion to theater and writing. It is a newer resource and growing, but also promises to act as a very solid networking resource for those in the arts with its Millennium Art Forum section.

http://www.arts-online.com/default3.htm

NATIONAL MUSEUM OF AMERICAN ART Here one can sample the thousands of art objects archived by what is considered the nation's first federal art museum. Also available are museum publications and a glance at current and past exhibitions such as the "White House Collection of American Crafts."

http://www.nmaa.si.edu:80/

OTIS A top, top art site. This is an eclectic but comprehensive Web compilation of current arts endeavors, ranging from cyber-displays of painting, sculpture, and photography to computer-generated images and "body" art. Of itself, OTIS says: "OTIS at its most basic, interpretation and intention, is a place for image-makers and image-lovers to exchange ideas, collaborate, and in a loose sense of the word, meet." The word OTIS stands for "Operative Term is Stimulate."

http://sunsite.unc.edu:80/otis/

PLAYBILL ONLINE This publication is considered one of the topmost authorities on the theater industry. Here you will find a very complete theater listing and ticket availability section. And it goes without mention that there are reams of interviews with theater people and personalities.

http://www.webcom.com/broadway

SCREENWRITERS & PLAYWRIGHTS This page is tailored to the needs of those who provide our favorite actors with the words they speak. It attempts to cover all aspects of the profession, from dramatic structure to marketing. This site includes links to complete scripts, lyrics to musicals, and tips from the "pros."

http://www.teleport.com/~cdeemer/scrwriter.html

PHYILLS' BROADWAY At Phyills' one will find not only play listings but also summaries of shows. There is also a rundown of what's new on Broadway, off-Broadway, and in the touring companies. And you can book tickets through this Web page if you have a party of twenty or more.

http://www.onbroadway.com/index.html

THE SISTINE CHAPEL This is a sublime offering from the Christus Rex Web site, wherein the viewer is offered multiple views and perspectives of Michelangelo's ceiling masterpiece. Developed by Michael Oltenau, it offers hundreds of JPEG shots of the artist's aerial work, ranging from *The Creation* to *The Last Judgment.*

Also available through the Christus Rex page are literature and art from the famous Vatican Library.

http://www.christusrex.org/www1/sistine/

TECHNO-IMPRESSIONIST ART GALLERY Touring the many rooms of this gallery and reading the various selections offered, one can see the current genre of Techno-Impressionism in the process of ongoing definition. Many of the works available for viewing have transcended their digital and computer-generated origins to stand on their own as art.

http://www.digiweb.com/tkarp/

THEATER CENTRAL The avowed purpose of this site is to bring a sense of order to the various theater resources available on the Net. Central is comprehensive and contains information on unions, regional theater listings, amateur and community theater updates, and information on non-traditional theater. There is also info on playwrights.

http://www.mit.edu:8001/people/quijote/theater-central.html

UNIVERSITY OF MARYLAND ART GALLERY One can find a culturally rich collection of art and artifacts here, ranging from traditional African sculpture and Chinese ceramics to mid-twentieth century Japanese prints and American Social Realism.

http://www.inform.umd.edu/EdRes/Colleges/ARHU/
ArtGal/.www/aghome.htm

Women

Compiled by Lauren Crowley

THE ADA PROJECT Do you have a knack for the Net? Think this computing stuff is fun? Then click on The Ada Project, a clearinghouse of information and resources relating to women in computing. Located at Yale University, this page provides a central location for conferences, projects, discussion groups and organizations, fellowship and grants. Computing positions and career info make this a valuable site.

http://www.cs.yale.edu/html/yale/cs/hyplans/tap/tap.html

ATLANTA REPRODUCTIVE HEALTH CENTRE HOME PAGE Given the proper info, women can become active participants in their own health care and make better choices. The home page provides accurate material on infertility, endometriosis, contraception, sexually trans-mitted disease, menopause, stress management, and PMS.

http://www.ivf.com/

ASSAULT PREVENTION INFORMATION NETWORK The APIN con-tains information on martial arts, how to protect yourself and your children, how to choose a self-defense course, and violence in the home and workplace. Readers provide real-life self-defense stories and solutions.

http://galaxy.einet/galaxy/Community/safety/
AssaultPrevention/apin/APINindex.html

THE AFRICAN-AMERICAN HOME PAGE features a Singles Con-nection, where women can post and/or answer ads. The ads include interesting biographies, profiles, pictures, and e-mail addresses for further contact, if interested. This home page has African-American recipes and is sponsored by the *Successful Black Parent* magazine, which focuses on children from birth to adolescence and has relevant articles and info.

http://www.lianet.com/~joejones/index.htm

BABY WEB Need help naming your baby? BABY WEB carries baby-naming software at its Baby Web Store. There are FAQs, baby care and development, and Internet Babies with pictures and biographies of new people.

http://www.netaxs.com/~iris/infoweb/baby.html

BEIJING: U.N. WOMEN'S CONFERENCE Many of the proceedings at the United Nations Fourth World Conference on Women in Beijing during September 1995 were available through the Internet.

Over 185 nations sent representatives to this conference, with about 7,000 government delegates from various countries attending. Key issues discussed during the Beijing conference included equal access to employment, credit and equal pay for women; equity in health care; equal access to education; equality of government representation for women; and cracking down on rape and domestic violence. A variety of reproductive issues—including abortion rights—were on the agenda as well.

The goal of the U.N. member states attending the conference was to adopt a "Platform for Action" on these issues.

There was also an overlapping meeting of non-governmental organizations called the NGO Forum taking place in Beijing, with an estimated 39,000 women attending this gathering.

An "official" home page for the FWCW is being maintained by the UN and can be found at:

http://www.undp.org/fwcw/daw1.htm

The Linkages home page, maintained by the International Institute for Sustainable Development, has a great deal of background information in the FWCW meeting. Among other information available on the Linkages page is the entire "Draft Platform for Action and Beijing Declaration" which has been rendered into Web-readable hypertext.

http://www.iisd.ca/linkages/women.htm

BREAST CANCER INFORMATION CLEARINGHOUSE The New York State Education and Research Network is the host for this site, which lists everything you need to know about breast cancer, including tips on early detection, medical information, a listing of regional support groups, and a question and answer section. Also has publications from the American Cancer Society.

http://nysernet.org/breast/Default.html

THE DIVORCE PAGE This includes support groups for women like Mothers Without Custody (with a phone number to join) and Single Mothers by Choice home page (founded by a psychotherapist) that gives advice to single mothers.

http://www.primenet.com/~dean/women.htm/

EMOTIONAL SUPPORT GUIDE Click here for Internet resources for coping with physical loss, chronic illness, and bereavement (including miscarriage).

http://asa.ugl.lib.umich.edu/chdocs/support/general.html

FEMINA This site says it is the first World Wide Web-based directory containing information exclusively for and about women and girls on-line. In addition to sixteen main topics, there is search option that looks for links based on keywords. Young girls have a place at Femina, with a home page and information about grade, middle, and high schools.

http://www.femina.com/

FEMINIST MAJORITY FOUNDATION Click on the site index and get a two page index of links to related issues. The FMF home page helps visitors keep up with congressional activity on issues such as affirmative action, equal opportunity, and family planning.

http://www.feminist.org

GUIDE TO WOMEN'S HEALTH ISSUES This all-encompassing guide separates women's well being into emotional health, physical health, and sexual health.

http://asa.ugl.lib.umich.edu/chdocs/womenhealth
womens_health.html

HEALTHSITE This is your resource for natural health and holistic lifestyle information. The latest in natural nutrition and medicine is here, as well as ordering info.

http://www.healthsite.com/

JIM MANSFIELD'S This is an index of resources includes feminist issues, women's health, women's studies, and woman-related sites on the Internet. "Who is Jim Mansfield?" you may ask. He's a guy who works at the Institute of Biodiagnostics in Winnipeg, Manitoba, Canada, and who created this comprehensive listing.

http://www.ibd.nrc.ca:80/~mansfield/feminism.html

NATIONAL ORGANIZATION OF WOMEN The home page for the National Organization of Women lists general information and history of the organization as well as how and where to join your local chapter. NOW's Hot Topics categories include abortion and reproductive issues, lesbian rights, economic equity, violence against women, global feminism, and racial and ethnic diversity. Back issues of the monthly newspaper are available on-line.

http://now.org/now/

SISTERLOVE An AIDS/HIV support group for women, by women, that pays particular attention to African-American women. Sisterlove provides education, advocacy, and empowerment to women and their families.

http://www.hidwater.com/sisterlove/

VOICE OF WOMEN This organization's home page lists conferences and a calendar of events pertaining to women. If you prefer doing business with women, their Resources for Women of Vision showcases women's goods and services through a master directory.

http://www.voiceofwomen.com/

WOMEN ONLINE Amy Goodloe, the director of Women Online, a Macintosh and Internet consulting referral service for women, puts her own unique spin on her women's resource home page. In addition to links to feminist activism pages and mailing lists, she has "Hotlist" with a "Cool Site of The Day Archives" and "Weird Places on the Net."

http://www.best.com/~agoodloe/women.html

WOMEN'S RESOURCE MOSAIC PROJECT compiled by a group of women from the University of North Carolina, this site offers over twenty-four categories on women's studies and resources on the Internet. An alphabetical listing gives you links to a wealth of information, including links to the National Parent Information Network, a listing of Women's colleges, a Women's History page, and Women's Legal and Public Policy Information.

http://sunsite.unc.edu/cheryb/women/wresources.html

THE WOMEN'S HOMEPAGE From the Massachusetts Institute of Technology, this site includes links to topics such as Gender and Sexuality, Feminism and Political Activism, Women's Health, and Women in Academia and Industry.

http://www.mit.edu:8001/people/sorokin/women/index.html

WOMEN'S STUDIES The University of Maryland has an extensive women's studies database that includes conference announcements, employment opportunities, and film reviews. Useful biographies of women in Congress and where they stand on legislative issues are under the Government and Politics category.

http://www.inform.umd.edu:8000/EdRes/Topic/WomensStudies

LIFE TRENDS INTERNATIONAL Will you be one of the millions of Americans limited by aging, weight, or fatigue? Not if you click on Life Trends, which features programs That promote good health, weight management, and skin care.

http://mfginfo.com/lifetrends/lifetrends.htm

PREGNANCY & HEALTH EDUCATION INFORMATION Focuses on reproductive health and has links to pages regarding pregnancy, birth, and midwifery. There's ultrasound info from the National Institute of Health, pregnancy book reviews and The Breastfeeding Shop, your on-line stop for products and advice.

http://www.iglou.com/members/robin.html

SAFE SEX PAGE If you ever had a doubt what safe sex is, this page will answer all your questions and them some, including lesbian safe sex. Brochures, articles, and handouts are available, as well as a user's forum. Condoms (for men and women) get their own link and contain a wealth of info. A multimedia section takes the user through stock situations and provides safe sex solutions.

http://cornelius.ucsf.edu/~troyer/safesex.html

NATURAL FAMILY PLANNING Thinking of starting a family? The Natural Family Planning site gives an introduction to what it's all about. The basics, FAQs, books, and organizations are listed to help the visitor. NFP is compared to other methods in terms of effectiveness.

http://www.usc.edu/hsc/info/newman/resources/primer.html

THE LESBIAN HOMEPAGE is dedicated to promoting lesbian visibility on the Internet and lists organizations, products, and services as well as lesbian-owned businesses.

http://www.lesbian.org/

BISEXUAL, LESBIAN, AND GAY RESOURCES This virtual library is maintained by the UC Berkeley Multicultural Bisexual Lesbian Gay Alliance's Online Services Project and features listings of college and university servers, national and regional organizations, health-related servers and gay and lesbian on-line publications.

http://www.infoqueer.org/queer/qis/vl'queer.html

BISEXUAL RESOURCE LIST is maintained by the Bisexual Resource Centers in Boston and Edinburgh and has a calendar of events, mailing lists, newsletters, radio programs, and a product source list.

Gopher://una.hh.lib.umich.edu/00/inetdirsstacks/bisexual%3ahamilton

THE L & B WOMEN'S PAGE provides support for lesbians and bisexuals. Also includes The LGB Guide to Great Britain and contains general, national, and regional info.

http://phymat.bham.ac.uk/LGB/women.html

CARENET A network of care for women in crises, Carenet is a Christian, pro-life network of pregnancy care centers and churches and lists effective abortion alternatives.

http://www.goshen.net/CareNet

SINGLE WOMEN TRAVELERS can find out the best places to meet men in some of the world's most exotic locales at this site. Adventurous single travel writer Lori Morgan shares tricks, safety precautions, and articles. Morgan recommends certain Club Meds; there men outnumber women ten to one!

http://www.travelxn.com/women/homepage.htm

Also, the Globe Corner Bookstore in Boston publishes a newsletter entitled Women & Travel, which features articles by women travelers as well as relevant book reviews and ordering information.

http://www.gcb.com/catalog/

WOMEN'S WIRE This excellent page looks at many women's issues in an amusing way. Features include Women in the News, "Sylvia" comics, female quotes, a forum for backtalk, and women's businesses on the Web. A Q & A section answers users questions about sex, business, exercise, men, money, and fashion. Women's Wire is at:

http://www.women.com/~

CYBERGRRL Another fun site with snappy writing and hip things to do. There's lots of hyphenated links, including Biz-Line, Health-Wise, Info-Zone, and Family Life. A women's guide to a Cool Surf Page is included.

http://www.cybergrrl.com/

WOMEN IN MUSIC International Alliance for Women In Music is Internet support for women composers and musicians, and consists of a coalition of professional composers, conductors, performers, musicologists, educators, and librarians. Their mission is to "celebrate contributions of all women musicians, past, present, and future."

http://music.acu.edu/www/iawm/home/html

MUSE The journal of women in music; covers the best female musicians, singers, and songwriters in all genres of music, including rock, alternative, folk, blues/R&B, classical, gothic, and New Age.

http://www.val.net/VillageSounds/muse/index.html

WOMEN'S WAY Need some female bonding time? Women's Way invites you to "settle into a comfortable, overstuffed chair, take off your shoes, let down your hair . . . and make yourself at home." This page wants to provide a space where women feel safe and comfortable to speak their thoughts, feelings, and experiences and create an atmosphere for women to share and connect. Women's Way features artistic and literary expressions by women and publishes ideas and information relating to home and family, working life, leisure, health, healing, and spirituality.

http://www.omix.com/womens_way/womens_way.html

THE WOMEN'S FISHING PARTNERSHIP This organization thinks that women should have a chance to bond via fishing. Whether you are an old angler or want to learn, the WFP coordinates female fishing trips, provides information on your states regulations and licensing requirements, and provides you with everything you need to know for a rewarding trip.

http://www.eskimo.com/~baubo/wfp.html

FEMINIST SCIENCE FICTION, FANTASY & UTOPIA This page focuses on a subject that has traditionally been a male domain. This page concentrates not only on female science fiction writers, but any author who portrays strong women in nonconventional or untraditional roles. Stories include the retelling of traditional myths, fairy tales, and folklore from the feminist perspective.

http://www.uic.edu/~lauramd/sf/femsf.html

WOMEN'S RUGBY Dubbed "1995 Hot Sport" by *Rolling Stone* magazine, this site tells where to find a club in your area and lists a schedule of tournaments and scores of previous matches. E-mail contacts and a mailing list keep you connected in the rugby world.

http://vail.al.arizona.edu/rugby/uswrugby.html

WOMEN'S SPORTS PAGE If there's a woman playing a sport, it's on this home page which provides links to several activities, including water sports, weight lifting, volleyball, golf, gymnastics, biking, lacrosse, and motor sports. Gender equity and other issues are presented, along with a list of festivals around the world.

http://fiat.gslis.utexas.edu/~lewisa/womsprt.html

FEMALE BODYBUILDERS HOMEPAGE They're here to pump you up! Contains links for home pages of standout bodybuilders with photos and tips. Bodybuilding magazines and books are recommended and a schedule of upcoming contests is listed.

http://www.ama.caltech.edu/~mrm/body.html

WOMBATS If they're not there already, they're coming to a town near you. The Women's Mountain Bike and Tea Society sustains a women's off-road cycling network that helps members learn trails in their areas and improve riding skills. There's a WOMBArt gallery, calendar of events and conventions, and a listing of regional chapters.

http://www.wombats.org/

YOGA The Sahaja Yoga home page can help you discover your inner peace and equilibrium in all aspects of life. There's an introduction, "the message," events, and a list of Sahaja (which means "spontaneous") Yoga centers around the world. Learn to balance yourself

mentally, physically, emotionally, and spiritually.
http://www.cs.purdue.edu/homes/costian/sy/more.html

MOM'S HOMEPAGE Has home schooling tips and reference materials, a Tupperware on-line catalog, arts and crafts, The Family Room, and an on-line "game room" for kids with the Internet version of Lite-Brite.
http://www.mnsinc.com/medixon/momshome.html

CAREER Kansas Careers is not a listing for jobs in Kansas but a mentoring guide that contains nontraditional career resources for women, and includes The Interest Assessment for Women. By responding to 210 work activities, women can find career interest areas and focus on developing rewarding careers. There are links to other Internet career and educational information and resources, including financial aid.
http://www.ksu.edu/~dangle/

SCIENCE AND ENGINEERING Organizations, information, sites, documents, and profiles of pioneering women. This is an inspiring site even if you are not interested in science or engineering. Women and minorities in science and engineering:
http://www.ai.mit.edu/people/ellens/Gender/wom_and_min.html

BIZWOMEN This provides an on-line interactive marketplace for women in business. The goal is to communicate, network, exchange ideas, and provide supports via the Internet. For a fee, you can get your business on-line with your business card, brochure and/or catalog to make your services available all over the world. If you haven't started your business yet, there's references and resources on how to start your own business, including financing and advice.
http://www.bizwomen.com/

WEDDINGS Here the intrepid Internaut will find everything from wedding gowns to questions about who pays the wedding bills, as well as such topics as premarital counseling and the issue of the bride changing her name. The best wedding page we found had been put together by Sonja Kueppers, and was an outgrowth of the soc.couples. wedding newsgroup. Its address:
http://www.wam.umd.edu/~sek/wedding.html

Writing

Compiled by Greg Micklos

The World Wide Web is filled with many resources and cool sites for writers, from beginners to experts. Whether it's inspiration you're looking for or you just want to become a better writer, the Web has many resources available. You can read great works from Shakespeare to Kerouac. You can visit sights that have some of the up-and-coming writers or go back and time and discover some of the lesser-known writers.

The new kind of literary 'zines are on the web. You can take a class through e-mail or even get teamed up one on one with a tutor to give you feedback on your writing. You can visit you favorite authors' home pages or check to see if their books are on-line yet.

There are a number of Internet libraries on the Web, where you don't have to worry about being quiet or it not being open on weekends or holidays. You can even go to school; a number of colleges and universities have their writing centers up on the Web.

PROJECT GUTENBERG "Anything that can be entered into a computer can be reproduced indefinitely," that is the philosophy of Project Gutenberg founded by Michael Hart. Project Gutenberg's goal is to have ten thousand books on-line by the year 2001.

The Project concentrates on putting books that are in the public domain on-line. Donations, volunteer work, and "private obsessions" all work to get at least eight books on-line each month. Books by authors from Karl Marx to John Milton are already on-line. And the list keeps growing each month.

> http://www.aether.com/Aether/gutenberg.html

ALEX & THE CATALOGUE OF ELECTRONIC TEXTS In Alex one finds one-stop-shop for many of the thousands of electronic texts that have been placed on the Internet. The works available here are catalogued and cross-referenced by author and by text, and include texts that have been collected by such endeavors as Project Gutenberg, Internet Wiretap, and the On-line Book Initiative. These recourses are available in Gopherspace at the following URL:

> gopher://rsl.ox.ac.uk:70/11/lib-corn/hunter

BANNED BOOKS What do *Ulysses* and "Little Red Riding Hood" have in common? They both have been the objects of censorship and censorship attempts. There are other books that have made it onto "banned" lists across the U.S. and the world. What are they? Check out the Banned Books On-Line home page.

http://www.cs.cmu.edu/Web/People/spok/banned-books.html

BARLETT'S BOOK OF QUOTATIONS From Walt Whitman's *Leaves of Grass* to William Shakespeare's *Othello*, Bartlett's Quotations is the one stop to search who said what and when in the literary world. Also here is the Bible (Old and New Testament), and the Book of Common Prayer.

http://www.cc.columbia.edu/acis/bartleby/bartlett

BEATNIK FOREVER AT LITERARY KICKS It's been nearly a half-century since the literary world first discovered a group of writers from New York City known as the Beat generation. At the Literary Kicks site you can discover the words that helped define a new generation of American writers.

Literary Kicks is the creation of Levi Asher, a "thirtysomething" Wall Street consultant. The site not only provides a great historical background about the Beat generation and its writers (Jack Kerouac, Allen Ginsberg, and William S. Burroughs), but it also gives current information on events, conferences, and stories that are related to the continuing phenomena of Beatitude. The latter can be found in the Beat News section of this Web site.

Also available for reading from this home page is the 1952 *New York Times* article titled "This is the Beat Generation," that will help inform those who are new to the study of Beat literature. This article by John Clellon Holmes put this group of writers on the road map of American letters.

A visitor to this Web site can also read portions of the so called "bible" of the Beats—*On the Road* by Jack Kerouac. Or you can get a list of films about the Beats, find out about the connection between Beat literature and rock music, or read about the relationship between Buddhism and the Beats.

http://www.charm.net/brooklyn/Topics/BeatGen.html

BOOKWIRE Who says television and electronic publishing have killed off books?

The book business is alive and well and will hit $25 billion in sales this year. Bookstores are booming this fall, with a new crop of bestsellers. And one of the best Internet sites we have encountered is devoted to books, book reviews, links to libraries, and book publishers. It's called BookWire, and can be found at this address:

http://www.bookwire.com/

Founded by Jamey Bennett and recently acquired by Individual Inc., BookWire has information of value to book readers, writers, and sellers.

You can start by clicking on the *Publishers Weekly* bestsellers list for the current week and be rewarded with a list of the top fifteen books in various categories. Some of the titles are also linked to book reviews.

The best place for reviews, however, is the page's link to the *Boston Book Review*, a literary arts newspaper that reports on the national and international literary scene. The *Boston Book Review* page sorts its reviews into book categories.

■ Dead Author Society

Emily Dickinson Poems from 1896 are at:

http://www.cc.columbia.edu/acis/bartleby/dickinson

William Faulkner's home page is:

http://www.mcsr.olemiss.edu/~egibp/faulkner/faulkner.html

When James Joyce died in 1944, did we lose the greatest genius of all time? That's just one of the questions the IQ Infinity: The Unknown James Joyce home page tries to answer at:

http://www.mcs.net/~jorn/html/jj.html

The poems of nineteenth-century writer John Keats can be found at:

http://www.cc.columbia.edu/acis/bartleby/keats/

As kids we all read Herman Melville's *Moby Dick*. Now we all can re-visit *Moby Dick, Billy Budd*, and other great works by Melville at The Life and Works of Herman Melville at:

http://www.melville.org/

One of the all-time American classics is *Huckleberry Finn* by Mark Twain. On the Web there are exhibits, scholarly studies, scattered writings, syllabi, and other resources for teachers, all focusing on the life of Mark Twain.

> http://web.syr.edu/~fjzwick/twainwww.html

■ Libraries on the Web

While most people on the Web know it doesn't beat going to your local library and getting lost in the shelves, the Web offers various libraries that are open on weekends and holidays and in the early hours of the morning.

THE INTERNET PUBLIC LIBRARY The IPL (Internet Public Library) is divided—similarly to a regular library—into four sections: Reference, Youth, Services for Librarians and Information for Professionals, and the Education Division. The Education Division is divided into three main areas: the Building Directory, the Classroom, and the Exhibit area. To visit the Internet Library type.

> http://ipl.sils.umich.edu/

BOOK REVIEWS A great link to books and book reviews available on the Net.

> http://gs.sdsc.edu:70/1/SDSC/Genifo/Internet/books

THE LABYRINTH LIBRARY Middle English can be found at:

> http://www.georgetown.edu/labyrinth/library/me/me/html

■ Literature Pages

There are a number of pages on the Web dedicated to literary movements or special writings. Here's a sample:

WOMEN WRITERS Some of the best writers in the world are women. And to prove that, we have a home page that celebrates women writers over the centuries.

> http://www.cs/cmu.edu/Web/People/mmbt/women/celebration.html

BOOK STACK Want to know your favorite living author's e-mail address? Interested in science fiction books? Want to get the latest information on writers conferences? There's no better place to check out than in the Book Stack's Author's Pen home page.

http://www.books.com/author1/htm

KID'S BOOKS We all know that today's kids on the whole do less reading and more television-watching. But why not try to get your kids to read on the Internet? There's a great one-stop for Internet resources related to books for children and young adults.

http://www.ucalgary.ca/~dkbrown/index.html

■ Publishing on the Web

Today thousands of writers are discovering a new place to get their works published, the Web. There are many sites already on the Web, and many more being created to act as the modern printing press. There are also a number of groups that writers can join to help them get their work published on the web.

A good place for writers (both beginners and experts) to go first is back to school via university writing centers. Here's a sample.

THE UNIVERSITY OF MAINE Writing Center Online

http://www.maine/edu/~wcenter/resource.html

PURDUE Writing Lab Web Server Home Page

http://owl.trc.purdue.edu/

ST. CLOUD STATE University and LEO (Literacy Education On-line)

http://condor.stcloud.msus.edu/leo/

E-MAIL SCHOOL Classes are also available for a fee via e-mail on the Web. Some of the classes available include Introduction to Fiction Writing, Writing a Mystery Novel, and Script Writing. To find out about enrollment and fee, go to:

http://www.writers.com/

■ More on Publishing

When it's time to try to get your masterpieces published on the Web, there are a number of home pages devoted to publishing works from both beginners and expert writers. Here's a sample of "literary 'zines" on the Web.

THE ABRAXUS READER A bi-weekly literary publication. Works include fiction, poetry, political essays, and music reviews. The *Reader* pays for submissions. Back issues are also available.

http://www.nwlink.com/~vidiot.abraxus/

BEATRICE WWW A literary page with a Generation-X leaning. Fiction, poetry, and reviews.

http://www.primenet.com/~grifter/beatrice.html

THE BLUE PENNY QUARTERLY An international literary review that pays for good poetry and fiction.

http://ebbs.english.vt.edu/olp/bpq/front-page.html

DEPARTURE FROM NORMAL To many, this is the top literary 'zine home page. They say their mission statement could be "they do everything because they want to." They accept everything (as long as they like it!). Everything includes stories, poems, music, animation, original photographs, and other forms of art that can be digitized. They are particularly interested in work created by artists, authors, and musicians who are non-corporately sponsored.
http://www.teleport.com/~xwinds/dfn.html

ENORMOUS SKY Temple University's literary magazine on-line. It includes poetry, prose, art work, and photography all produced by the students of Temple University. It's a good page to check out some of the future of America.

http://www.music.temple.edu/Sky/

eScene eScene offers the best of the best in on-line fiction. The stories featured are an anthology of on-line fiction found from the electronic magazines published on the Web.

http://www.etext.org/Zines/eScene/

117

INTERTEXT THE ON-LINE FICTION MAGAZINE InterText comes out every two months. It's been around since 1991.

http://www.etect.org/Zines/InterText/

MADNESS As you can tell by the name, not your normal 'zine. Postmodern ideas that many who are into underground or different writings will enjoy. Includes horror fiction and poetry.

http://web1.trenton.edu/~domurat

MISSISSIPPI REVIEW An on-line monthly magazine that includes literary fiction, poetry, essays, commentary, and reviews. There is also information about literary competitions.

http://sushi.st.usm.edu/~barthelm/index.html

PIF *Pif* is a literary magazine for new authors. Submissions of short fiction, artwork, and poetry from beginners are encouraged. A great place to get your stuff published.

http://www.aloha.net/~lucks/pif/coming.html

VERBAL ABUSE A literary quarterly for the so called "culturally jaded." The magazine presents arts and letters in a different way, not afraid to shy away from sexual themes or works that are often unpublishable elsewhere.

http://mosaic.echonync.com/~interjackie/verbal/issue.html

■ Poetry

Poetry is alive and well on the Web. More and more home pages are popping up devoted exclusively to poetry. Here's a sample.

CLICHÉ A relatively new poetry and prose magazine that is now available on the Web. You can read it and submit your own work too.

http://www.mbhs.edu/~dchase/cliche.html

BREAKFAST SURREAL A link to poetry on other people's home pages.

http://www.indirect.com/user/warren/surreal.html

SO IT GOES Claims to be the first Web page devoted solely to poetry.

They are looking for both known and unknown poets.

http://www.pitt.edu/~soitgoes/1/option1.html

THE WRITE PAGE An on-line newsletter for readers and writers of genre fiction. Romance, historical, science fiction, fantasy, mystery, horror, and paranormal genres, plus author listings of their past, current, and coming books.

http://www.writepage.com

History

AMERICAN MEMORY Those wishing to view an excellent multimedia exhibit dealing with American culture and history, go here. Many of the photographic images are nothing short of spectacular, and evoke the past for the viewer in a most haunting manner. There is an interactive form that users can fill out to search the thousands of photos available. Shots range from the Civil War to the work done under the direction of the Farm Security Administration. This is part of the Library of Congress archive.

http://rs6.loc.gov/amhome.html

THE AMERICAN CIVIL WAR

"There is no escaping history." —Abraham Lincoln

While there are a number of university pages covering this topic of continuing obsession to modern Americans, a good general starting point for research is B. D. Boyle's collection of excerpts from Civil War-related books and documents. Entire books available for reading include the *Red Badge of Courage* and the moving *Life of Frederick Douglas*. Documents range from Lincoln's first and second inaugural addresses to his famous Gettysburg Address. There is also writing from Mark Twain, letters from Civil War soldiers, and the words to a bittersweet Irish song of the era—"Kathleen, Mavourneen."

http://www.access.digex.net/~bdboyle/docs.html

Louisiana State University is working on the creation of a database of all private and institutional holdings of various materials from and about the Civil War. This Internet locale also has myriad links to other Civil War historical sites.

http://www.cwc.lsu.edu/

BENJAMIN FRANKLIN This is a good primer for those boning up on old Ben Franklin. While not a scholarly site, this Internet locale is good for schoolkids who want to know more about this particular founding father.

http://sin.fi.edu/franklin/rotten.html

GEORGE WASHINGTON PAPERS This is an ongoing project at the University of Virginia to compile and catalog the papers and correspondence of "The Father of Our Country."

http://poe.acc.Virginia.EDU/~gwpapers/GWhome.html

GOPHER HISTORY JEWELS While the Net address below is for a Web page (i.e. http), this is actually the gateway to some excellent Gopher menus. The topics range from Alaskan historical documents, Hellenic Civilization, and the Holocaust to space at the Johnson Space Center History Archive.

http://galaxy.einet.net/GJ/history.html

HISTORY COMPUTERIZATION PROJECT This is a large-scale undertaking between the University of Southern California, the Los Angeles City Historical Society, and the Conference of California Historical Societies, to build a history information network between historians, libraries, archives, museums, preservation groups, and historical societies. You will find links to all these types of groups through this resource, and the scope of the project is worldwide including similar groups across the planet.

http://www.direct.net/history

or:

http://www.history.la.ca.us/history

HISTORIANS GUIDE TO E-MAIL AND INTERNET RESOURCES Compiled by Marc Becker at the University of Kansas, this page is just what it says it is.

http://history.cc.ukans.edu/history-dept/internet/guide.html

NATIONAL TRUST FOR HISTORIC PRESERVATION The National Trust is an organization with more than 250,000 members. As the leader of the national preservation movement, the National Trust is committed to saving America's diverse historic environments and to preserving and revitalizing the livability of communities nationwide. This home page will tell you all about the trust and give you information on the preservation efforts taking place in all fifty states of the U.S.

http://www2.nthp.org/trust/index.html

NATIONAL ARCHIVES The documents and catalog resources available here via the Internet are nothing short of immense, and growing.

gopher://gopher.nara.gov

VATICAN EXHIBIT Go into the previously hard-to-visit stacks of the Vatican Library where now, courtesy of the Internet, you can read and view rare and interesting manuscripts. Starting at the main hall of the exhibit, one can travel to "rooms" by subject, including archaeology, humanism, math, music, and medicine. The JPEGs of the actual manuscripts qualify as both art and history in their own right.

http://sunsite.unc.edu/expo/vatican/exhibit/Vatican.exhibit

WWW FOR HISTORIANS This is a well-compiled set of links to computer servers the world over that play host to historical information and databases. As such, this is an excellent jumping-off point for your research; almost any topic of history you may be interested in probably has a link here. Connections to servers include university history departments and resources in Europe, Africa, Australia, and the United States.

http://grid.let.rug.nl/ahc/hist.html

Religion

There is an abundance of religious material in cyberspace. When we went looking on the Internet, we were overwhelmed with the volume and variety of religious-oriented items we found. There are religious sites placed on the Net by church organizations, scholars, and universities.

AHAVATH ACHIM SYNAGOGUE This New Bedford, Massachusetts synagogue has been in continuous service for over one hundred years. And now it has a Web locale.

> http://www.ici.net/cust_pages/hartman/hartman.html

CAMPUS CRUSADE FOR CHRIST A dynamic Christian site designed to help people understand God's love and forgiveness, and build them in their faith.

> http://www.crusade.org

RELIGION COMMUNITY This particular home page on the Web is a good place to start researching religion. At this location there are seven categories to choose, including Buddhism, Christianity, Islam, and Judaism. There are also directories pointing to religious collections at numerous colleges and universities.

> http://galaxy.einet.net/galaxy/community/religion.html

RELIGION ARTS AND HUMANITIES Here we found these four major topics: Comparative Religion Studies, Mythology and Folklore, Scripture and Commentaries, and Theology. There were also nearly thirty document collections, grouped by such subjects as "A Guide to Christian Resources on the Internet," "Philosophy and Religion" from the Library of Congress, and "Info on Catholicism."

One can reach this location by clicking on the hypertext title at the Religion Community home page. Or it can be reached at this address:

> http://galaxy.einet.net/galaxy/arts-and-humanities/religion.html

CATHOLICISM The information on Catholicism here was assembled by Carnegie-Mellon University. This site is host to numerous documents, ranging from Papal Encyclicals over the centuries to documents concerning Vatican II which overhauled the Catholic Church in the mid-1960s. Also available were home pages on the World Wide Web that have been created by the Catholic dioceses of Mobile, Pittsburgh, and Raleigh.

> http://www/cs.cmu.edu:8001/web/people/spok/catholic/html

GUIDE TO CHRISTIAN RESOURCES There are eight categories of Christian resources located at this site, including those available via e-mail, FTP, the World Wide Web, Gopher servers, Bulletin Boards, and Usenet Newsgroups. Creators of the site write that the guide is for Internet users interested in "`Classical Christianity,' a term coined by C. S. Lewis to describe a theology which affirms the importance of a transforming faith in Christ as God and Savior."

Among the resources listed were dozens of newsgroups and List-servs, dealing with everything from theology to missionaries. Instructions are provided on how to subscribe.

http://www.iclnet.org

This guide is also available via gopher at:

gopher://gopher.mc.edu

Travel

The Internet is a fertile source for an Internaut looking for travel and tourism information, or for booking a trip in the real world.

AIRLINES AND AIRPORTS This site lists all, or almost all, Internet sources of information on airports and airlines. Also, many travel-industry sites are linked here.

http://www.bekkoame.or.jp/~dynasty

BUSINESS TRAVELER Here you will find country-specific information for fifty countries for international business travelers. Information is excerpted from *Craighead's Business Reports*. This page is designed to help ease the strain of long-distance travel in order to conduct business successfully, worldwide.

http://www.craighead.com/craighead

GNN TRAVELER CENTER After checking out many of the Internet's travel resources, we decided one of the best is the Global Network Navigator (GNN) Travelers Center. The center gives you a wealth of choices, and the best one to start on is "Internet Resources" which takes you to a page packed with hypertext links on all manner of travel subjects. There are sections on visas and passports for foreign travel, languages, transportation, things to do at travel destinations, and lodging.

http://gnn.com/gnn/meta/travel/index.html

AESU TRAVEL AGENCY If you want information on low-cost airfares, a travel agency called AESU has a homepage on the Web which is valuable. At this location, you punch in the name of the airport you are departing from, and AESU gives you a range of airfare prices to various foreign and domestic destinations.

http://www.charm.net/~aesu/flight.html

FLORIDA TRAVEL PAGE For information in general about Florida and its various attractions.

http://204.31.16810/travel/florida/

STUDY ABROAD This in an on-line source of information on college study aboard programs. At the last count they had listing for four hundred different educational opportunities. Also, this page links directly to many home sites for study abroad programs.

http://www.studyabroad.com

TORONTO This page says it is Toronto's home on the World Wide Web. And indeed it seems that if there is a Toronto-based or oriented link on the Web, this page has a link to it. All encased in a high-speed, high-quality user interface.

http://cyber-yonge.com

TRAVEL USENET GROUPS For the real lowdown on low-cost travel, it's best to plug into one of the numerous Usenet newsgroups that concern themselves with travel. Here are several of the best:

rec.travel.air

rec.travel.marketplace

rec.travel

There is a lot of activity at those newsgroups from people telling about their trips and passing along tips. But there is also heavy traffic from individuals and travel agents anxious to sell air travel and cruise tickets at rock-bottom prices.

The usenet newsgroups are also a great place to learn something about the people and culture of a travel destination, according to travel writer Allen Noren. Read the soc.culture newsgroups for the country you plan to visit or write about, e.g., soc. culture.ireland. Also go to the newsgroup news.answers which has the FAQ list from various news-groups. Most FAQs provide at least a history of the country, the ethnic groups that live there, where to go, and what to expect.

LAS VEGAS Get into the family car along with the kids and mother-in-law and take a motoring vacation somewhere in the good old USA. Las Vegas is a popular destination; it's got an extensive Internet presence.

http://www.infi.net/vegas/online/

NICARAGUA This is said to be the land of lakes and volcanoes. At this page you will find that and more, including poetry, news, general information, music, art, literature, food recipes, law, politics, and links to other Nicaragua-related sites.

http://sashimi.wwa.com/~roustan

ORLANDO Another leading travel destination, especially for families with young children, is Walt Disney World in Florida. To learn about accommodations, attractions, shopping, tours, and of course, Disney World.

http://www/magicnet.net:80/orlando/

WINE COUNTRY For information on the wine country north of San Francisco, including both of the premier wine-growing locations, Napa Valley and Sonoma County.

http://www.freerun.com/napavalley/mwinerie.html

For Sonoma County use this address:

http://www.geninc.com/gen...ma/travel/index.html

Sports

The two media heavies on the sports scene—ESPN and Time Inc.'s *Sports Illustrated*—both have excellent sites on the World Wide Web. But top-flight sports sites are also maintained by many other groups, and by such special interest groups as the National Football League.

ESPN In terms of usage, ESPN's "SportsZone" Web site consistently ranks near the top of all World Wide Web home pages. This underscores the fact that nearly 80 percent of Netsurfers are males, who tend to be sports fans. It has become so popular that publisher Geoff Reiss moved on August 28, 1995 to divide the site into one fee-based area and one which will continue to be free. The home page offers headline sports stories which change daily, a news wire, a special Major League Baseball link, and a half-dozen daily features which consist of news, analysis, and commentary.

The day we browsed the site in late August, there was an excellent team-by-team preview of prospects for the new NFL season, complete with votes by Pro Football Weekly staffers on the strength of each team.
http://espnet.sportszone.com/

SPORTS ILLUSTRATED This magazine, among others, can be found at Time Inc.'s "Pathfinder" site, which also has links to the company's other magazines and to numerous hot news topics.

Once you arrive, click on the *Sports Illustrated* cover and you will be connected to the magazine's first-rate Web site. Under the "News" category, one first gets headlines and links to a dozen top sports stories of the day. There are links to special news sections dealing with football, baseball, golf, basketball, and other sports. The day we examined the site, under football were links to college football stories, NFL stories and statistics, and Canadian football.
http://pathfinder.com

THE NFL The National Football League has its own Web site called "Team NFL." At the NFL site, you will find areas for each team with information from club officials; the official NFL news wire which includes injury reports, transactions and statistics; an NFL library with an on-line rule book and record book; and a game day package with up-to-date information about all the on-the-field action.
http://nflhome.com/temp-nfl/teamnfl.html

THE RALEIGH (NC) NEWS AND OBSERVER This is one of the most respected Web sites among the nation's news media, and its "Nando-Net" includes excellent sports sites under the heading "Sports Server." The regular baseball section has American and National league categories, and within those categories are special sections dealing with the Eastern, Central, and Western divisions. At the top of the page is a daily news section, and at the bottom of the page are links to any kind of statistic a sportswriter or commentator would ever want.

The football section of the Sports Server has separate professional and college categories, as well as a search tool which enable users to locate hard-to-find data.

http://www2.nando.net/SportServer/

LEISURE & RECREATION Probably the most comprehensive Web site dealing with sports is maintained by EINet Galaxy. Their "Leisure and Recreation Sports" site is simply immense because it includes participatory sports as well as the armchair events favored by middle-aged sports fans.

The opening menu lists forty-six separate sports categories, starting at air hockey and ending with wrestling, and including hang gliding, rugby, and snooker, along with the major sports.

There are also collections of sports articles and data in various categories, links to other sports sites on the Web, and several discussion groups.

http://www.einet.net/galaxy/Leisure-and-Recreation/Sports.html

JAWS The ultimate football Web site is called "Jaws," which stands for "Just Another Web Site," but it is a lot more than that. It is a collection of all known links to Web sites pertaining to pro football. It has NFL scores and stats, a news and information section which includes a lot of opinion pieces helpful to sports columnists and commentators, and an "Adults Only" section with the odds and point spreads on up-coming contests. But its unique section consists of links to every home page of each team in the NFL.

http://www.earthlink.net/~dbsofw/nfl/

SPORTSLINE This is sports service with a heavy commercial element, aimed at parting sports fans from some of their money. Promoter Mike Levy assembled a number of sports celebrities as advisors and content providers, including Joe Namath and TV personality Bob Costas for the site's debut in mid-August. It opens with the usual collection of top sports stories of the day and a scoreboard for results. There is a section called "The Press Box" that provides opinion, analysis and commentary from some of the world's leading sportswriters. There's also a "Mall of Fame" where fans can buy sports items.

http://www.sportsline.com

■ Golf

GOLFWEB This site is a commercial operation and the most comprehensive of the two golf sites we examined. Everything is free for the Netsurfing sportswriter, but the site does carry some advertising and material from golf vendors.

GolfWeb has five main sections. "What's New" has the latest items which have been posted to the site, including press releases from major golf organizations around the world. "Tour Action" has all the results and statistics from major golf tours, updated as they happens. "Places to Play" includes information about golf courses and resorts worldwide, and there's also a place to access the Worldwide Encyclopedia of Golf Courses which can provide important insights for the golf writer doing a piece about a tourney at a specific course. There is also the "GolfWeb Library" and the "GolfWeb Pro Shop."

http://www.golfweb.com

GOLF ARCHIVES The second golf site we visited was Golf Archives, run out of Princeton, New Jersey and available both by Gopher and the World Wide Web. At this site there are about a dozen selections on the opening menu. They include selections on how to calculate golf handicaps on your PC or Mac and how to keep track of golf statistics, as well as a section on club making. You can also access "GolfData On-Line," which is described as a complete electronic golf bulletin board which offers an updated golf library, golf travel service,and pro shop.

gopher://dunkin.princeton.edu/
http://dunkin.princeton.edu

■ Soccer

INTERNATIONAL RESULTS AND CLUBS This home page by Bob Pak contains connections to soccer-related sites all over the world. One expert says this has the best connection to soccer clubs worldwide of any Net resource.

http://www.pitt.edu/~ktgst/international.html

FEDERATION INTERNATIONALE DE FOOTBALL ASSOCIATION (FIFA)
To many this is the most significant soccer organization in the world, and here you can find what the need to know about the World Cup.

http://wc94/oslonett.no/wc94/fifa.html

RETE! This an international soccer page from Italy, which features nearly 2,000 photos, 1,200 teams, 6,000 players; matches, charts, and news updated everyday. The page is bilingual.

http://www.vol.it/RETE-/homerete.html

USA SOCCER KIDS This is an entertaining and fairly comprehensive site with lots of information for younger soccer aficionados.

http://www.cts.com/browse/jsent/kid.html

■ 1996 Olympic Games

GUIDE TO THE 1996 OLYMPIC GAMES This is the official home page of the Atlanta Olympic Games, and boasts the best graphics, design, and sound bites of any of the related sites. It is, however, a bit heavy on the sponsorship angle and often reads like a running advertisement.

http://www.atlanta.olympic.org/

IT'S ATLANTA! THE OLYMPICS This page is updated regularly, and has several interactive features, such as maps. There are information links to national team sports and organizations, venues, and training sites.

http://www.com-stock.com/dave/

THE ATLANTA CONSTITUTION JOURNAL As one of the "hometown" newspapers for the city that is hosting the Olympics, the *Journal Constitution* site features Olympic related articles. Its "Weekly Update" follows the progress of planning for the event. There is also information on tickets, events, and venues.

http://www.ajc.com

Business

ADVERTISING AGE This is the well-known standard of the advertising industry—*Advertising Age* magazine.

http://www.adage.com

ADVERTISING RESOURCE GUIDE This business school-based guide has links to many sources of information on the advertising and marketing field.

http://www.missouri.edu/internet-advertising-guide.html

AMERICAN MARKETING ASSOCIATIONS This the professional trade association for those in the marketing business.

http://www.ama.org

■ Investment

Huge banks, stock brokers, and investment firms have elaborate sites on the World Wide Web, along with hundreds of smaller outfits trying to make a buck by providing financial services in cyberspace.

We visited a number of the locations and, especially for the bigger financial firms, found Web pages of high quality that bulged with information. Much of it was aimed at individuals with money to invest.

EDGAR One of the most valuable Internet locations is the New York University "Edgar" project, which involves putting invaluable corporate financial information from the Securities and Exchange Commission onto the World Wide Web in a manner that makes it easy to retrieve and read.

Operated by the NYU business school under grants from the National Science Foundation and other supporters, the Edgar project is a must-stop for information seekers looking for the inside scoop on the business world.

http://edgar.stern.nyu.edu/edgar.html

FIDELITY Most of the big investment houses have a major presence on the Web, including Fidelity, the nation's number one mutual fund company. At the Fidelity home page, an attractive, somewhat formal site, a variety of information and financial tools are available for the business reporter as well as the investor. There's even a "Contests and Games" department to lighten up the place.

Among other things, you can use an asset allocation worksheet, review mutual fund performance data, order a fund prospectus, or get a demo copy of Fidelity software which can be used to place orders for stocks and mutual funds and obtain price quotes.

http://www.fid-inv.com

MERRILL LYNCH At this site, investors can learn about Merrill Lynch products and services, obtain generalized financial advice, and read a "Special Report" from the firm's research department about the current investment climate.

http://www.ml.com

STREETNET There are a host of other, smaller investment entrepreneurs on the Web offering information, products, and services. One of the most comprehensive is StreetNet. There are separate sections for corporate profiles, stocks, mutual funds, daily market news, and weekly market summaries, as well as a section on financial magazines. You can also input the symbol of your favorite stock and get an instant price quote.

http://www.streetnet.com/home.html

INVESTMENT USENET SITES While dealing with investment professionals is one way for the Internaut to obtain information, other useful sources are the Usenet news groups on the Internet. Here are some of the better ones to check out with your news reader:

misc.invest.stocks (for stock news)
misc.market.biz (for general market information)
misc.invest (for general investment news)
misc.invest.funds (for mutual funds)

■ General Business Information

THE WALL STREET JOURNAL This Net version of America's top financial newspaper features timely business news, information on companies and corporations, and stock quote information.

131

http://www.wsj.com

BIZ INFO AT KENT STATE This is one of several colleges that have assembled impressive collections of information of value to business internauts.

At this location, select Gopher menu item #3, "Business Sources on the Net," and you will be introduced to a cafeteria of resources, starting with accounting and including economics, finance, investments, management, and personnel. Before you start browsing, be sure and read menu selection #2, "An Introduction to BSN," which tells how the site is organized, how to use it, and how to download files you want.

To get there, point your Gopher to:

gopher://refmac.kent.edu

UNIVERSITY OF MICHIGAN Those who need specific state economic background information can obtain a summary of state-level economic data collected by the Department of Commerce. Direct your Gopher toward the University of Michigan using the following Gopher address:

gopher://unan.hh.lib.umich.edu/11/ebb/summaries

Also at the U of M you can find GSPs (Gross State Product: a total of all goods and services for each state) at this Gopher address:

gopher://una.hh.lib.umich.edu/11/ebb

■ Corporations—A Quick Trick

There's one all-purpose address on the World Wide Web that will give you access to the home pages for numerous companies. The address is:

http://www.name of company.com.

For example: If you insert "IBM" for "name of company," you will arrive at the IBM home page on the Web.

■ The Labor Market

Everything from economic data on the health of the economy and the level of unemployment to the job outlook for this year's crop of high school and college graduates is available on the Net.

There are also a multitude of sites where job hunters can post their resume and where companies can list the job openings they are trying to fill.

But like everything else in the vast, uncharted territory of the Internet, it's best to have a road map before you venture into cyberspace in search of a employment information. In preparation for this story, we asked the Web Crawler searching tool for sites containing job information, and the tool found 3,342 locations.

DEPT OF LABOR Much economic data and documents about the labor market are located at the U.S. Department of Labor, whose address via the Library of Congress is:

gopher://marvel.loc.gov:70/11/federal/fedinfo/
byagency/executive/labor

BUREAU OF LABOR STATISTICS The BLS at the DOL is where you will find all the employment information. You can go directly to the BLS by Gopher or on the World Wide Web. Those addresses are:

gopher://stats.bls.gov:70/1
http://stats.bls.gov/

At the BLS there is the full text of the monthly employment-unemployment report, of course, along with state and local statistics on employment and unemployment. But there's also a helpful section which puts recent trends in the American labor market into historical perspective.

If you are wondering about the job outlook for various occupations, access the Labor Department via Gopher and go to the annual "Occupational Outlook Handbook" which is on-line and is one of the menu choices.

AMERICA'S JOB BANK There are numerous Net sites that try to match job seekers with job openings. Many are operated by colleges and universities as a service to graduating students and alumni. Still others are commercial enterprises that charge fees either to employers or job seekers. However the largest such service, called "America's Job Bank," is operated by the federal government in cooperation with the fifty state employment services across the nation.

http://www/ajb.dni.us/

ONLINE CAREER CENTER This seems to be the oldest and largest commercial employment service on the Internet. At this location individuals can post resumes and conduct job searches for a fee, and corporate recruiters can list job openings and examine prospects on-line, also for a fee. The service is free to colleges and students. There are also pointers to other career-related databases.

http://www.iquest.net.occ/

CATAPULT Many individual colleges and universities have their own Internet sites to help students find jobs through advice, career information, and job matching. This is a collaborative effort called "The Catapult," involving several colleges.

http://www/wm.edu/catapult/catapult.html

■ Legal Issues

If you want to research specifics of the law, check government regulations, verify a U.S. Supreme Court decision, or peruse the United States Code, then there's something on the Internet for you.

CORNELL UNIVERSITY Start with the Legal Information Institute at Cornell University. In a peculiar aberration from most World Wide Web sites, the Internet address at Cornell starts with the word FATTY instead of the more common WWW syntax.

http://fatty.law.cornel.edu/

As one enters the hallowed, legal cyberhalls of Cornell there is no question—at least for this reporter—of having struck a legal jackpot. Among the available resources are a hypertext front-end of recent Supreme Court decisions (distributed the day of the decision under project Hermes), and a Web version of the full U.S. code.

The Supreme Court site has handy cross-referencing of decisions under topical subject headings that range from Abortion, Firearms, and FOIA, to Habeas Corpus, Harassment, Indians, Insurance, Military, and Workers' Compensation.

There is also a subject listing in the Main Menu section of the

Cornell legal home page which allows for access to legal materials either referenced by Legal Topic, (such as Constitutional Law, Copyright) or by Type or Source (Treaty, Legislation).

Other information links at this Cornell home page include the National Center for State Courts WWW Site, Copyright Clearance Center, Constitutions of the World, the Library of Congress Server, and a link to the American Bar Association.

A resource is also provided for looking up lawyers on the Internet.

VIRTUAL LAW LIBRARY Another good Internet spot to begin any type of legal research is at the Virtual Law Library, which is brought to you by Indiana University Law Library. Here you will find an alphabetical listing of law schools and law firms, and more importantly, you will find legal material that is organized by topic and type of source.

http://www.law.indiana.edu:80/law/lawindex.html

ADVERTISING LAW For those interested in the fine points of Advertising Law, the Washington-based law firm of Arent, Fox, Kintner, Plotkin, & Kahn boasts just such a resource. The site is maintained by firm lawyer Lewis Rose.

Advertising law information at this Internet site includes such items as the Federal Trade Commission's proposed telemarketing regulations and regulations from the Fair Packaging and Labeling Act, Fair Credit Reporting Act, and Magnuson-Moss Warranty Act.

http://www.webcom.com/~lewrose/home.html

REAL ESTATE Now let's get back to something more pedestrian, like the real estate business and its resources on the Web. Here you will find a menu-driven Web site that allows the user to search for information by state and then by city. Searches can also be conducted by price.

http://www.homes.com/realestate/exist.html

Government and Politics

While the Internet spans the globe, as far as "government" goes, we focus on just the U.S. government in this section. This is based on the assumption that most of our readers will have a similar focus. We have

135

provided a hierarchical listing of resources that begins with two of the most important—the White House and Congress—and listing below each the various resources connected with those two entities. For instance, starting with the White House, we jump to the various executive branch agencies that come under presidential authority.

WHITE HOUSE This is a good starting point for any government research. The White House has a substantial amount of information resources, and you can jump from this Web site to all the federal agencies.

At the White House Web site, one is greeted with "An Interactive Citizen's Handbook" that gives virtual tours and has information on the first family.

Click on the icon for The President's Cabinet and you'll find the home pages of the fourteen agencies that fall under the executive branch of government. All of the agencies have current news, applicable legislation, publications, periodicals, and up-to-date press releases concerning that particular department.

http://www.whitehouse.gov/

■ Some of the Departmental Agencies

AGRICULTURE This department manages our national forests, protects our soil and water, helps farmers and ranchers, and improves food safety among other things. Also within Agriculture's purview is the administration of agricultural exports and keeping foreign plant and animal diseases out of the United States.

http://www.usda.gov

COMMERCE This agency is not just about trade. Commerce's broad range of responsibilities include granting patents, predicting the weather, measuring economic growth, promoting minority entrepreneurship, and overseeing the U.S. Travel and Tourism Administration.

http://www.doc.gov

Also within Commerce is the Census Bureau, which for some represents such a goldmine of statistical information. We give it a longer review next.

CENSUS BUREAU The Census Bureau has a Web site with numerous menu choices. Most Internauts will want to select the Main Data Bank, which takes you to the heart of the statistical information the Bureau has on the Internet. There, your selections include such items as Census Bureau News Releases, the Statistical Abstract of the United States, International Trade Statistics, Population Data, County Business Patterns, and an intriguing selection entitled "Data Access Tools."

We selected the Tools item and found that one easy tool was a graphical map of the United States. If you want population data from Ohio, for example, you click your mouse on Ohio and at once get a statistical profile from the Buckeye State. And if you want data from a particular county, you go to the map of Ohio's eighty-eight counties, click on the county you want, and are quickly presented with a thirty-section statistical profile of the county.

http://www.census.gov/

or:

gopher://gopher gopher.census.gov

File Transfer Protocol: ftp ftp.census.gov. Log in as "anonymous" and use your complete e-mail address as the password. Once connected, change to the "pub" directory by typing "cd/pub."

Questions about accessing Census on-line are handled by Public Information Officer Liane Rozzell at 301-763-4051. On request, she will fax you a complete sheet of on-line instructions. Her fax number: 301-457-3670. Or e-mail to pio@census.gov

DEFENSE Want a fresh quote from the secretary of defense? Need to know if the National Guard unit in your town is on the Pentagon's new hit list? Require details of the new defense budget? That's all here at DefenseLINK, where the Internaut will find each of the four branches of the U.S. Armed Forces—Army, Navy, Air Force, Marines—as well as each of the myriad offices of what is the largest of the bureaucracies in government. The DefenseLINK Locator allows one to easily search through a database of defense-related information.

http://www.dtic.dla.mil/defenselink/

EDUCATION For the education researcher, there are ample Internet resources at the U.S. Department of Education.

Available resources include the newly reauthorized Elementary and Secondary Education Act; "Strong Families Strong Schools," a new report based on thirty years of research about parent and family involvement in education; "Moving America to the Head of the Class: 50 Simple Things You Can Do"; and numerous other research reports and education statistics.

Also at Education are pointers to other education resources on the Internet, including the National Parents Information Network and over seven hundred software programs that range from teaching ABCs to calculus lessons.

http://www.ed.gov/

or by using Gopher at:

gopher://gopher.ed.gov.

E-mail users can reach the Department's catalog and Mail Server instructions by addressing mail to almanac@inet.ed.gov and then typing "send catalog" in the message block of your e-mail screen.

ENERGY From the Department of Energy home page, you can search for expert contacts within the DOE on a variety of topics. And there is a large volume of energy-related documents and publications you can peruse.

http://www.os.dhhs.gov/

ENVIRONMENTAL PROTECTION AGENCY The mandate of this organization needs little explanation. EPA operates a solid, straightforward site where the embattled federal agency explains its role and provides reams of documents outlining its activities. Everything from press releases to sections on EPA rules and regulations is here. There is also a search window near the top of the Web home page, where one can type in the subject of their inquiry and be directed to the specific EPA location where it can be found.

http://www.epa.gov

■ Congressional Data

THOMAS Congress has launched a on-line service called THOMAS to deliver legislative information via the Internet.

Named after Thomas Jefferson, this service makes available the full text of any bill introduced since 1992, along with all the new legislation the resurgent Republicans and morose Democrats drop in the hopper this year. It also has the e-mail addresses of House and Senate members who use e-mail, and Web home page addresses for those congresspersons who are "wired."

Also, THOMAS will soon offer the Congressional Record, the daily report which caries every word uttered on the House and Senate floor.

http://thomas.loc.gov

CAPWEB This is one of your best entry points into U.S. government information. CapWeb is an Internet window into the minutia of Congressional workings, it can provide information on bills, congressional e-mail addresses, Hill home pages and even an Internet link to the General Accounting Office.

"It is the product of a couple of impatient Capitol Hill staffers who felt it was an effort worth undertaking and don't mind writing some html (Hypertext Markup Language) late at night," says CapWeb's opening disclaimer. "CapWeb is designed to be an effective means of providing information about Congress and links to related internet resources via the World Wide Web." The culprits responsible for helping to put Congress further into the Internet limelight are Hill staffers Chris Casey and Jeff Hecker.

http://policy.net/capweb/

C-SPAN America's premier unfiltered news cable, which for several years has been showing citizens how government works by simply having open cameras on Congress and other news events, now has a top-notch Web site dealing with government and politics.

http://www.cspan.org

■ Environment

It's been a quarter of a century since the environmental movement exploded into public consciousness. Today, headlines are being generated by political efforts to roll back some of the environmental laws of previous years.

Those following this ongoing story will find valuable material on the Internet. There are a number of solid, straightforward Internet sites posted by government agencies and old-line conservation groups, as well as exciting and argumentative postings by environmental activists.

ENVIROWEB One of the best environmental resources found by us is EnviroWeb. A project of The EnviroLink Network, it is a volunteer, nonprofit organization which bills itself as the "largest on-line environmental information service on the planet," reaching 550,000 people in ninety-eight countries. It was created in 1991 by Josh Knauer, then a freshman at Carnegie-Mellon University, and is still head-quartered there.

The opening menu on the EnviroWeb home page has links to an environmental library, a mailing list archive, an environmental forum, and to an immense Internet Environmental Resource Directory. Each week, EnviroWeb features two special sites, and the week we visited they featured a Salmon link and a Forests link dealing with logging of old-growth redwoods.

At the EnviroLink library, there are selections on environmental issues, activism, organizations, and publications. And there's an "EnviroGovernment" link which lists environmental information by governments at all levels, including state, county and city.

http://www.envirolink.org/

It can also be accessed by Gopher, at this address:

gopher://envirolink.org

ECONET Operated by the Institute for Global Communications, which is an activist group claiming 10,000 members that operates three other computer networks known as PeaceNet, ConflictNet, and LaborNet, in addition to its environmental EcoNet.

At EcoNet, the opening Gopher menu has numerous selections, including those dealing with climate, environmental law, pesticides, toxic wastes, and a guide to other Internet environmental resources.

http://www.icg.apc.org.igc/en.html

WILDERNESS SOCIETY This is one of the old-line conservation organizations. The opening page of the society's Web site features an attractive graphic of Balanced Rock in Arches National Park, with a low-key description of the Wilderness Society, founded in 1935, with 300,000 members today and an annual budget of $16 million, dedicated to improvement of America's national parks, forests, and wildlife refuges.

There are several dozen links dealing with timber sales, forest fires, Mining law, wetlands, Yellowstone, and the Everglades, among others.

http://town.hall.org/environment/wild_soc/wilderness.html

■ Health

THE CENTER FOR DISEASE CONTROL This is the federal agency on the front line in the fight against infectious disease, and it is also a magnificent source for anyone interested in health in general. Perhaps most important for those who want to keep on top of health problems and disease outbreaks around the nation, the weekly CDC "Morbidity and Mortality Weekly Report" (MMWR) can be downloaded from the agency via the Internet.

Also available is a rundown on the CDC's eleven constituent agencies, which include a health statistics center, an infectious disease center, OSHA, and the national immunization program.

When we first accessed the site in late May 1995, the "What's New" section contained Ebola information, as well as press releases on a variety of subjects that had recently been issued by the CDC. We punched up the Center for Infectious Disease and were presented with the CDC Disease Information page. Choices ranged from Plague Information and Tuberculosis to Hospital Infections. Accessing the Hospital Infections provided a menu with sixteen choices on types of infections that can break out in hospitals. It also told how to how they can be avoided or combated.

The CDC home page menu choice entitled "Publications, Products, and Subscription Services" brings Internaut to the justly renowned "Morbidity and Mortality Weekly Report." There are instructions on how to download the MMWR, along with the free Adobe Acrobat software required to read it.

In addition to offering access to all the CDC's own resources, the CDC home page also has pointers to other health resources on the

Internet. These include the Canadian Medical Association, the Communicable Disease Surveillance Centre in the UK, the National Library of Medicine HyperDOC, the Federal Department of HHS and the World Health Organization. It also points out any state health departments that are currently on-line.

http://www/cdc.gov/

■ Social Security and natural Disasters

SOCIAL SECURITY ADMINISTRATION On the third day of every month, more than 46 million Americans receive total payments of more than $28 billion from the federal government.

The vast majority of these beneficiaries are collecting Social Security checks, but about six million are getting the funds under a Supplemental Security Income program which helps the very poor, aged, and disabled.

The Social Security Program, which enrolls 133 million people in the active work force and pays benefits to fully 16 percent of the American population, was created in the depths of the Great Depression and has become a popular political sacred cow. It has so far escaped the Draconian cuts being inflicted on federal programs by the new Republican majority in Congress, but it is certain to come under scrutiny after the 1996 presidential election.

At the Social Security Administration home page one can check on their own Social Security account and find out about their own potential retirement benefits.

The "Office of Research & Statistics" section should prove of value to any researcher. That's where all the hard data is located, including "Fast Facts," state breakdowns, and information about Social Security programs elsewhere in the world.

Elsewhere on the SSA home page, users can download any one of several dozen basic Social Security publications. They are in the PDF typeset format, and you need to download the available, free Adobe Acrobat software to read them.

If you don't want to handle it that way, there's an easy provision for you to send an e-mail requesting a specific publication, and Social Security will promptly send you the publication by return e-mail.

And for the benefit of that new baby in your house, Social Security also can download the form needed to get him or her a Social Security card and number.

http://www.ssa.gov/

DISASTERS The 1990s are proving to be the decade of natural disasters. The Federal Emergency Management Agency home page on the World Wide Web is a solid resource for anyone with questions about natural disasters. The home page itself is organized by accessible titles like, "I Want to Know," "Help After Disaster," and "News Desk." Topics range from general information about disasters to how to apply for disaster aid, and press releases are available.

There is also a good collection of documents on mitigation, or the prevention of further damage after the initial disaster. "Recovery Times," a hard-copy publication for disaster victims, is available on-line. A new page under construction will house the revised federal disaster-response plan. The Master Index provides an alphabetical listing of all documents available.

The Disaster Response Fact Sheet covers the human aspects of surviving a disaster. Readers find out how to locate safe drinking water and maintain a sanitary shelter in emergency situations. The fact sheet includes a section on helping children cope with emergencies, discussing issues such as keeping the family together or identifying when a child needs professional help.

One passage advises, "Although it might seem to make more sense to leave a child in a safe place while looking for housing assistance, children may become anxious that parents might not return." The document goes on to encourage parents to include children in the cleanup, as well as building the temporary shelter.

Although FEMA operates exclusively in the USA, this information on the Internet benefits disaster victims anywhere in the world. Mark Wolfson, a FEMA spokesman, noted that after the Kobe earthquake, there were almost 2,000 visits from users in Japan.

http://www.fema.gov

■ Police

Through the Internet you can plug into police agencies ranging from the U.S. Department of Justice to the London Metropolitan Police

Department. And perhaps even more importantly, you can take a close look at hundreds of local police departments.

All this information is a natural stop for researchers looking for information about crime patterns, police techniques, or just about the criminal justice system.

CRIMINAL JUSTICE REFERENCE SERVICE One of the best starting places for police and crime-related research is the Justice Department Information Center of the National Criminal Justice Reference Service. Billed as the most extensive information source in the world on criminal and juvenile justice, it's a clearinghouse serving all bureaus of the U.S. Justice Department.

At that location there are buttons you can click to get data about prisons, courts, crime statistics, drugs, juvenile justice, and international crime.

When we examined the site in mid-September 1995, the "What's New" section had a new report on alarming juvenile crime trends, a report on the amount of damages awarded in civil trials during the past year, and a report on a new drug control strategy.

http://ncjrs.aspensys.com:81/1/new2/homepage.html

POLICE RESOURCE LIST This has links to local police departments around the U.S. and abroad as well as links to federal and state law enforcement agencies and college campus police departments. It is at this site that one can jump to the London Metropolitan Police Department. But you can also take a look at small town police departments as well as those in the nation's big cities.

We clicked on the Ft. Myers, Florida and got a picture of the police headquarters and a menu listing local police services, local police phone numbers, and answers to frequently asked questions. There were also several public service sections, dealing with how citizens can protect themselves from crime. We also clicked on the Chicago Police Department home page where we found a welcome message from the mayor, an explanation of the city's new community policing initiative, and some reports on local crime trends. The address of the Police Resource List is:

http://police.sas.ab.ca/prl/index.html

COMMUNITY POLICING For those interested in the growing trend toward community policing, there is a rundown on the Chicago Police Department's Chicago Alternative Policing Strategy (CAPS) on a special page.

The CAPS page acts as an extension of the department's community policing program. It answers questions about what the program is, tells how members of the community can get involved, and gives schedules for "Community Beat Meetings" where beat cops and residents meet to talk about local crime.

There is also news on the page, such as a report on the decrease in Chicago homicides so far this year, an announcement about changes in the 911 system, and a Hate Crimes Report.

Chicago's community policing page is at:

http://www.ci.chi.il.us/Chicago/html/caps/caps-wn.html

CECIL GREEK CRIMINAL JUSTICE PAGE Another excellent police Web site is maintained by Cecil Greek, a criminology professor at the University of South Florida. His Criminal Justice Page has numerous links to crime-related Web pages, including one to a searchable police database.

Topical links through the Greek page range from Drug and Alcohol Information, Prison, the Death Penalty, Criminal Justice and the Media, and Due Process and Civil Rights.

Also included are links to Supreme Court decisions, on-line criminal justice discussion groups and the FBI's Law Enforcement Bulletin.

http://www.stpt.usf.edu/~greek/cj.html

■ Politics

By the time this book hits the bookshelves the presidential and congressional campaigns will in full swing. This promises to be a great campaign year in terms of the battle of ideologies that is currently taking place for the heart and soul of the American voter. The following are some places to go for keeping informed:

ALLPOLITICS Early in 1996, *Time* magazine and CNN launched this estimable site, which takes an in-depth look at American politics. It has comprehensive content in the form of timely articles and news analysis supplied by the excellent staffs of both Time and CNN.

http://allpolitics.com

THE JEFFERSON PROJECT This place is one of several top political resources on the Net, with an extensive amount of information offered on anything and everything involving the art of politics. It boasts an extensive set of links to the home pages of national and local candidates; to the various party organizations—both state and local—and to relevant on-line magazine, political watchdogs, and to political humor.

http://www.stardot.com/jefferson

POLITICS USA With the credibility of the *National Journal* magazine and the American Political Network behind this site, it offers solid, bipartisan content that takes a continually updated look at the American political scene. Comprehensive features of this site include a searchable database of the famous "Almanac of American Politics."

http://PoliticsUSA.com/

POLITICAL SCIENCE A Net resource built by Peter Adams, a political science graduate student (perhaps graduated by now) at Trinity University in Connecticut. Entitled "The Political Scientist's Guide to the Internet," this Internet political tome is a bonanza for both the information it provides and the fact that it has winnowed down the available information to make the Guide more intelligent and intelligible.

The five basic categories in Adams' Guide—U.S. Federal Government Resources, U.S. State Government Resources, Political Research, Political Issues & People, and International Affairs—lead to a myriad of useful information resources.

The State Government link is especially helpful because it takes you to a list of forty of the states which have an on-line or Internet presence. One simply clicks on the state and is instantly connected to its on-line resources.

Through the Fed links you can quickly go to the White House WWW site, the agencies, the Library of Congress, and the Interactive

Citizens Handbook. The State Government area contains a lengthy list of state government resources, categorized alphabetically by state.

The Guide's International Affairs area links directly to a Web page maintained by Wolfgang Schlor as part of the University of Pittsburgh's International Affairs Network. The Issues & People listings contain links to political issues, politicians, political parties, and interest groups.

http://www.trincoll.edu/pols/home.html

International

THE WORLD BANK The World Bank home page is an extensive collection of information for researchers interested in the Bank. It includes sections on publications, the Public Information Center, private sector development, African development studies, the newly instituted Inspection Panel, and the Electronic Media Center.

In the publications section, you can browse through the Bank's catalog of books, studies, journals, and CD-ROMs. You can even order available materials. The Public Information Center offers such difficult-to-find items as Staff Appraisal Reports and environmental reviews of Bank projects. There is also information on Bank procedures.

Private sector development is currently hot in the lending world, so it is no surprise that it has one of the more extensive sections nested inside the Bank page. In it, you will find materials on the World Bank's efforts to support the privatization of government monopolies, particularly in the countries of the former Soviet Union.

Also of current interest is the Inspection Panel, an investigative body designed to ensure that the Bank follows its own social and environmental guidelines in project lending. There you will find a copy of the first case before the body, regarding the controversial Arun hydroelectric project in Nepal. The World Bank home page should provide interested parties with a whole new source of information on the little-known international institution.

http://www.worldbank.org

WASHINGTON'S EMBASSY ROW For Internauts who are also international affairs buffs, there is now an Electronic Embassy program which makes available the Washington diplomatic staff of many different countries.

Launched by D.C.–area firm called TeleDiplomacy Inc., the avowed purpose of this new Net site is "to link the staffs and resources of the embassy community to their constituencies in business and industry, education, the press, and government."

In addition to an indexed set of embassy links to each of the program's member countries, the site has a centralized virtual press office, an education office with information on student exchanges, and a consular office with information on passports and visas.

There is also a travel and tourism office, an employment office, and links to the cultural scene in the nation's capital.

TeleDiplomacy is an Internet consulting group based in Arlington, Virginia, headed by Ross Stapleton-Gray, who was a member of the White House Information Infrastructure Task Force. Gray also serves as president of the Washington, D.C. chapter of the Internet Society.

http://www.embassy.org/

SARAJEVO "But although death is all around us, we girls still try to look good. Our way of fighting is to look beautiful and to show those beasts that are killing us that youth and life will triumph over death."

These haunting words are an excerpt from Sarajevo On-Line, and were written by eighteen-year-old Alma Duran. She is a high school student and works as an English translator for an independent radio operation called "Station 99."

This and other messages are an example of a window onto the Bosnian conflict opened by the Internet. For those wishing to read these messages, and to speak with residents of the war-torn city of Sarajevo, an e-mail message can be sent via a service aptly named the "Sarajevo Pipeline."

The pipeline was officially inaugurated in spring 1995 as part of an effort "to promote dialogue between the inhabitants of Sarajevo and the Internet community," according to Ivo Skoric, who has written the introductory comments for this resource.

In addition to these moving, firsthand accounts from the war, the pipeline site contains numerous links to other information about the conflict. There is also a gripping exposition of photos from the war, representative of the many talented photojournalists who have been covering the story.

To find these resources about the former Yugoslavia, turn your browser toward the following URL:

http://MediaFilter.org/MFF/SJidx.html

■ More Balkans

There are many other sites dealing with the Balkan crisis. One of the top places for keeping posted on war news is CNN's Web page on the crisis.

http://www.cnn.com/WORLD/Bosnia/index.html

NATO has an excellent Gopher menu of press statements that can provide good background information to those researching the subject. The address:

gopher://marvin.st.nato.int:70/11/yugo

To keep current on U.S. Department of Defense announcements regarding Bosnia (and DOD news within the entire scope of departmental affairs) there is DefenseLINK. Its URL:

http://www.dtic.dla.mil/defenselink/

Mario Profaca, a Croatia-based freelance journalist, has created Mario's Cyberspace Station, which has a number of links to news and events in the former Yugoslavia.

http://jagor.srce.hr/~mprofaca/mcstation

■ International Trade Data

Did you know that in June 1995, the United States of America did a total trade volume (imports and exports) of $23.24 billion with its northern neighbor, Canada?

Well now you do, courtesy of data harvested from the Internet.

Internauts who follow that vast global movement of goods and services known as world trade can use the Net to obtain valuable information.

Business itself is still a novice at using the Net for communication and international business dealings, but there are several nascent efforts in this direction and a wealth of trade data from government sources.

DEPARTMENT OF COMMERCE Starting with the U.S. Department of Commerce and its various offices, one can locate anything from breaking press releases on trade to individual commodity trading statistics.

The Foreign Trade Division of Commerce's Bureau of the Census has a breakdown of the top ten trading partners with the U.S., an overview of government's international trade program, International Trade Reports and press releases, a Guide to Foreign Trade Statistics, and a Who's Who in Foreign Trade.

To help with information-gathering and for those who need quotes many of the Commerce Department resources including press releases, contact names, and telephone numbers.

You can find the Foreign Trade Division on the World Wide Web at:
http://www.census.gov:80/ftp/pub/foreign-trade/www

Another source of trade data at Commerce is the Economics and Statistics Administration, which is host to STAT-USA, a singularly informative Internet source.

STAT-USA bills itself as "The one-stop Internet source for business and economic data," and it is. It is the home of the National Trade Data Bank, Economic Bulletin Board, The Global Business Opportunities Service, and the Bureau of Economic Analysis.

The Data Bank alone can give you such trade information as export opportunities by industry, country, and product; the demographic, political, and socio-economic conditions in hundreds of countries; and even "how-to-market" guides for those seeking business tips.

To find STAT-USA, go to:
http://www.stat-usa.gov

One caveat: you can take a free test drive on STAT-USA, but there is a nominal fee for regular users. For further information on STAT-USA, call (202) 482-1986.

Also at the U.S. Department of Commerce is the International Trade Administration.

Like STATS, the ITA Net site provides access to the National Trade Data Bank (but without a fee). Also, there is trade information by country, region, and by industry.

In the ITA's Hot Issues and Announcement section one can find listings and background information on various trade shows and initiatives taking place throughout the world—for example there is currently a link to information on the U.S. Trade Mission to Northern Ireland, set for October 1996.

http://www.ita.doc.gov

UNITED NATIONS For official trade information outside of the scope of U.S. government agencies, there is the United Nation's Web site with its links to the UN International Trade Center and to the UN Conference on Trade and Development (UCTAD).

Of particular interest to those looking for business information is the UN's Trade Point Development Centre.

http://www.unicc.org/

EUROPEAN UNION For other trade-related information outside of the American perspective, there is the European Union home page with its links to member countries.

http://s700.uminho.pt/ec.html

TRADE COMPASS A private Internet effort designed for businesses and organizations engaged in international commerce is the Trade Compass Web site.

The main sections of the Compass home page include Trade-News, a summary of top trade stories; Marketplace, which acts as an international trade yellow pages; Trade Library; and Trade Forum, which aims to foster a dialogue between buyer and seller.

Note: There is a fee for some of the information offerings on the Trade Compass, though much of it is free or advertiser-supported.

http://www.tradecompass.com/

MARKET LINK A similar, but not as comprehensive, trade reference is the Market Link Web page.

http://nwlink.com/marketlink

151

UNIVERSITY OF MICHIGAN In the realm of academe, the University of Michigan Library Gopher is one of the premier sources of Internet accessible information on every topic imaginable, including trade. There is a comprehensive set of Gopher menus with such topical areas as International Market Insights, Foreign Trade, Best Market Reports, and Agricultural Situation reports that span the globe.

gopher://una.hh.lib.umic.edu:70/11/ebb

news

ANNOTATED GUIDE TO US MEDIA a.k.a. "Kurt Fliegel's Web Media Guide," this is a good, annotated, and oftentimes opinionated guide to U.S. media. It covers print press, TV, radio, magazine, and on-line news services. While a solid site in many regards, this is a one-person effort, and some of the annotations and content are out of date.

http://www.mcs.net/~kfliegel/media/media.html

BRITISH BROADCASTING COMPANY Before there was CNN, it was the BBC which was known the world over for its global coverage of news events. And even with CNN, the BBC is still one of the top, most respected news organizations in the world.

http://www.bbcnc.org.uk/worldservice/index.html

BOSTON GLOBE This is an ambitious Web site that lives up to its ambitions as a source of information not only for Bostonians, but for those throughout New England. In addition to the excellent content that one gets daily from the *Globe* there is also a searchable database of classifieds and regional information.

http://boston.com/globe/glohome.htm

EDITOR & PUBLISHER This is the top-notch trade journal of those in the newspaper profession. In addition to news about the news profession, this Web site has links to hundreds of on-line editions of newspapers across the country. Also included are many college newspapers.

http://www.mediainfo.com

CNN The respected cable television service has now established a top site on the World Wide Web which embodies many of the features that have made its video product so popular.

Called "CNN Interactive," the Web site's opening logo enables Netsurfers to click on ten different types of news, including U.S. News, Business, World News, Sports, Politics, and Showbiz. Also, the CNN Web site has a "Search" engine which will examine CNN's own database to find requested items. We asked it to find anything dealing with Medicare, and it came up with quite a few links to earlier CNN stories on the subject.

http://www.cnn.com/

CONGRESSIONAL QUARTERLY If you are a reporter who just can't get enough government information, log onto the Gopher put up by *Congressional Quarterly*, the weekly publication which is the bible of Washington correspondents.

Among items available are the lead stories from the CQ weekly report, a weekly news brief from the CQ research department, and when Congress is in session, a status report on major legislation.

gopher://gopher.cqalert.com

NEWSLINK This organization bills itself as the Web's "most comprehensive on-line news resource." It provides access to both newspaper and broadcast news home pages, as well as magazine sites. At our last count, it had more than six hundred newspapers linked to its page, and 425 broadcasters.

http://newslink.org

PATHFINDER This is a top news and popular culture locale, which is part of the Time-Warner Empire. Among other resources at the Pathfinder site, you can read *Time* magazine, *Sports Illustrated, Fortune, People, Southern Living*, and *Money* magazine. The topical search capabilities through the Pathfinder Web pages are top-notch.

http://www.pathfinder.com

ONLINE NEWSPAPER DIRECTORY This is a Web locale, devoted to compiling a linked directory of those newspapers that offer an on-line edition.

http://marketplace.com/e-papers.list.www/

SAN JOSE MERCURY NEWS This is probably the single best cyberspace edition of any newspaper in the world. Perhaps, though, this is fitting, because this paper is based in California's famous Silicon Valley. As the on-line adjunct to the print version of the Mercury News, this cyberpaper not only has comprehensive scope but also makes use of the new medium afforded by the Web in interesting ways.

http://www.sjmercury.com/

USA TODAY America's premier national newspaper, sold at corner stores, newsstands, and news boxes everywhere.

http://www.usatoday.com

WALL STREET JOURNAL The media has been full of Internet-related financial news. Now, in addition to reporting Internet news, the *Wall Street Journal* has created an Internet-based publication with the debut of the Money and Investing Update cybersection. The Update is a fully realized electronic publication that literally updates its news and stock quotes during the day.

Financial news junkies or just those in need of checking clippings from the *Journal* will find this an excellent source of business information. The look and feel of the Update is much like the print version of the *Journal*, with a What's News column, and a centerpiece story covering the markets. Click on a typical news brief and bang you jump to the inside page where there is a full news story on the topic in question. Other features include Company Briefing Books, which have detailed reports available on thousands of companies.

According to a spokesperson for Dow Jones & Company, which owns the *Journal*, the Update is the first step toward developing a full interactive edition of the paper by sometime in 1996. A note to potential readers: this resource is free as of now, but requires users to fill out a subscription form stating who they are. Plans are for a fee-based service during 1996.

http://update.wsj.com/

Alternative

BOOK OF BITTERNESS Here you will find the posting from USENET Newsgroup alt.bitterness. This is, indeed, a bitter collection of postings.

http://www.webfeats.com/sealander/Bitter_Book.html

BLADE RUNNER "He say you Brade Lunner." This is the vintage 1982 *Blade Runner* souvenir magazine in HTML format. There are three hundred images from the movie, production art, drawings, and sketches. And there are interviews with the filmmaker. Also, there are links to other *Blade Runner* sites.

http://www.wit.com/~xtian/blade_runner.html

COOL SITES (OF THE DAY AND YEAR) The Spot was chosen as "Cool Site of the Year" for 1995, after extended voting by the citizens of the Internet who selected this Web site in final elimination.

Tens of thousands of votes from thirty-six countries were cast during the summer-long process to select the top site from the hundreds which had appeared at InfiNet's well-known "Cool Site of the Day" page.

And the winner was The Spot, a site that is a gateway to the sometimes raunchy goings on at a typical California beach house with a cast of guys and dolls. They narrate activities to the Web audience through "intimate" diary entries and other means of communication.

A year ago, InfiNet Special Projects Coordinator Glen Davis, of Norfolk, Virginia, came up with the idea to select a daily "Cool Site."

"We were sitting around the office and I said to my boss, `Why hasn't somebody ever chosen a cool site of the day?'" Everybody in the office agreed it was a good idea, and Davis was handed the task of picking a new site every day.

Davis said that he takes this task "pretty seriously," and is "really pretty choosy."

Some of his previous choices have gone on to great Internet fame and have even lead to profits for the creators of those sites.

When it came to choosing a "Cool Site of the Year," the matter was left to public consideration, in keeping with the often populist nature of the Internet. Davis picked the top five sites, and then asked his fellow Internauts to vote on what site would take the grand title for the year.

"All five of the sites were my favorite, so I decided to let the rest of the world decide," Davis said.

And so the world did.

Davis said that he singles out "Cool" sites—including the top five—based on the sophistication used in the programming skills for the site; along with the imagination quotient, graphic arts, and the actual content of the site.

Runners-up in the "Site of the Year" contest included: Mr. Showbiz, an entertainment industry site; The Crash, a comic book, techno-anarchist site; Rocktropolis, a entree to all things rock-and-roll; and the Casbah, the most individual and haunting of the sites, with its multi-colored Marilyn Monroes and dire statistics about women in the modern world.

All these sites can be viewed by jumping from the Cool Site of the Day, page at the following URL:

http://www.infi.net/cool.html

INTERNET UNDERGROUND MUSIC ARCHIVE The Internet Underground Music Archive, known affectionately as IUMA is a page with 1950s diner-esque decor and a host of unknown nineties bands under the auspices of a capella, ambient, college, indie, rave, experimental, new age, progressive rock, reggae, ska, spoken word, surf, and thrash soul (whew).

Since most of this stuff isn't on the shelves at your socially-acceptable record store, bands like Baby Snufkin, Vincent's Ear, Grease Weezer, and Mooseheart Faith get their publicity.

http://www.iuma.com

IUMA also offers the FANCY PANTS wallpaper link, with twelve groovy patterns to download (free, of course) for your Web Browser or desktop at:

http://www.iuma.com/IUMA-2.0/pages/wallpaper

■ Punk Rock

The typical hacker is not the only one on-line today. Yes, even those who are labeled as outcasts to society have found their way onto the

World Wide Web. Punk rockers are just one example of the so-called "freaks" who have found their way onto the Web.

It seems like every punk with a computer has created their own home page so that everyone on-line can get acquainted with their favorite bands.

Using the Web Crawler is the most effective way to browse through the information on punk. However, if you just want to get to the good stuff, go directly to:

PUNK PAGE This page, designed by Jon Aizen, has a catalog of sounds, pictures, and home pages for almost all of the bands loved by punkers. Aizen created all of the bands' home pages himself, and there are over one hundred bands listed on the page. He also lists his e-mail address, so if you have any questions about his page or punk in general, he will get back to you very quickly. This page is incredibly popular. In the last month it has been visited by almost ten thousand users.

http://turnpike.net/metro/punk/index.html

If you want a second best hot spot, Victor Gedris' WORLD WIDE PUNK PAGE is the place to go. This page is a catalogue of home pages that bands have created for themselves. This page does not have nearly the same amount of resources that the PUNK PAGE has. There are, however, a few bands that cannot be found on the PUNK PAGE that can be found here.

http://wchat.on.ca/vic/wwp.html

■ Really Got to Rave

After the clubs close, ravers from around the world head to their computers to chat on the Internet. The World Wide Web has plenty of listings of where raves are taking place around the globe.

Brian Behlendorf created a page ready-made for information seekers: "all you wanted to know about raves but were afraid to ask." Although the font on this page is bland, the page does incorporate a lot of information. After the general information on raves is presented, as well as media references to raves, there is a listing of home pages. Those home pages from around the world serve as links to chat lists that you can subscribe to. These lists are unmonitored and can act as spots to find out about what really went on at any particular rave. Links to other, more insubstantial pages can be found here as well.

http://hyperreal.com/raves/

FUTURE CULTURE An on-line mailing list where you can reference information on raves and other issues about the future of society. This list is unmoderated. From this mailing list you can access information that may be useful to describe the culture surrounding the rave scene.

http://futurec.xtc.net/subscribe

■ The Wine Page

This is for the oenophile in the family and contains many links to the increasing number of wineries on the Internet.

http://augustus.cssr.washington.edu/personal/bigstar-mosaic/wine.html

■ Some Electronic Magazines

URBAN DESIRES Many consider this electronic offering *très chic* as a sophisticated cultural showcase that follows many of the artistic, musical, and travel hot spots on the World Wide Web. Desires bills itself as "an interactive magazine of metropolitan passions."

http://desires.com

THE VIRTUAL MIRROR When it first started, the *Virtual Mirror* was a ground-breaking magazine publication both because it was totally electronic and because it had advertising.

Written by hypertext journalists, the *Mirror's* editorial copy includes everything from Internet software reviews and movie reviews to gardening tips—there is even a "Fractal Gallery" for those so inclined.

"For now our content is weighted toward the WWW and the Internet," says Robert Stewart, the editor/publisher of the *Virtual Mirror*. "We hope to make the *Mirror* more appealing to a wider audience by constantly broadening the subjects covered."

He cites the quickly-growing demand for "new types of information and forms of expression" on the Internet as his reason for launching this endeavor.

"The *Mirror* doesn't aspire to be the on-line equivalent of a newspaper or magazine," Stewart says. "We are attempting to create a new form for a new medium, the World Wide Web."

http://mirror.wwa.com/mirror/

■ Other Alternatives

BANGKOK METRO MAGAZINE IndoChinaNet, Bangkok, Thailand.

An on-line version of *Bangkok Metro Magazine*, featuring an alternative look at the city and its people.

http://www.icn.net/icn/METRO.html

BEATTHIEF Stories and pictures about jazz, beat poetry, blackmail, plagiarism, shoplifting, and perjury. "More flava than a burrito."

http://www.beatthief.com/

CHRISTIAN SINGLES A computerized, global matching service dedicated to connecting interested parties with potential Christian mates, with special emphasis on matching beliefs and individual specifications.

http://www.christsingles.com/Two4Christ/

COURTNEY LOVE There is often no greater homage than that paid to a performer by an individual obsessed fan, some would say. At this Web locale there is everything one could hope to know about Courtney Love and her band Hole, all lovingly compiled.

http://www.albany.net/~rsmith/hole.html

THE E-MAIL CLUB An international group of men and women who enjoy exchanging e-mail.

http://www.emailclub.com

PHuNC NeT Here one will find loads of information about hacking, security, phreaking, anarchy, exploring systems, and more.

http://ocala.com/phunc/

THE PRONOIA PAGE This Web page is devoted to the concept of Pronoia ("the suspicion that others are conspiring behind your back to *help* you"). Pronoia came to prominence and international attention after a *Wired* magazine cover story on "Zippies" in 1994. The Zippies (Zen-Inspired Pronoia Professionals, or "hippies with zip") have some loose affiliations with the international rave scene and with the Rainbow Family of sixties holdovers. They are considered to be the ideological opposites of the slacker, Gen-X types who are seemingly overdrawn at the First National Bank of Resentment with their do-nothing, don't-care attitude.

The Pronoia site has a superlative collection of links to music, politics, and various virtual communities.

http://myhouse.com/pronoia

SPUNK MUSIC FANZINE This Web site specializes in punk and indie music. Here one can read about Sebodah, Magic, Dirt, Weezer, Liz Phair, and Flying Saucer Attack.

http://www.usyd.edu/au/mwodman/spunk.html

■

CHAPTER 8

The Way of the Cybrarian: Making the Internet Meaningful

by Suzanne Kincheloe

T he Internet—often called "the library without a card catalog"—provides a hobby, and sometimes a job, for many people trying to make sense of the Internet for the rest of the world. For the last few years, increasing numbers of information specialists (including all types of specialties) have been taking up Hypertext Markup Language (HTML) and the designing of home pages to aid with research.

These cyber-librarians or "cybrarians," as we'll call them, perform the traditional library tasks of gathering, selecting, and organizing information for a specific user or client base. While critics complain about the mediocre and chaotic content on the Internet, these cybrarians are laying the groundwork for a meaningful cyberspace by organizing material in their interest area or for an organization.

Building the Internet Toolkit

Most cybrarianship starts out as an organic enough process—a librarian creates bookmark files on his Web browser to have easy access to links he uses most often to answer reference questions. In the business world, one might collect the URLs of one's competitors to track press releases, product development, and other background information. It's clear, then, that the Internet has specific uses for individual organizations and workers, but trying to navigate through over 15 million individual pages on the Internet can prove tedious and even counterproductive. Thus the thrust to create the "work page," or a home page tailored to the research needs of an individual or an organization.

Developing the work page follows a similar process to the organizing of a traditional library or information center collection. One should discern what the user base needs and organize it in such a way that the information can be found efficiently. This chapter will explore the key questions to be asked when planning and developing a work page Web site, offer some design suggestions that will save time in locating information, and finally, discuss the administrative issues that can arise as a result of producing a successful and dynamic work page.

Planning the Home Page

The most important consideration in planning a research home page is discerning what the mission is. An effective home page anticipates what the user is looking for and where they will tend to look for it. The first step in planning your URL collection is to think about the missions and goals of your organization and the department or group using the home page. If the main goal of the work page is to create the kind of service that most fits the organization's goals and mission, then the corollary goal should be to provide only those Internet resources that support the information needs of the people using the page, also known as the "user base." In other words, the home page should act as a filter to the Internet, providing subject access and global access (search engines, broad subject directories, etc.).

The solo researcher may well have an intuitive idea of what should go on their home page. But, if you're working in a group, then planning should be a collaborative effort to ensure that all the best resources are included and the layout of the page is understood by everyone using it. The planning process should identify the most effective research tools known to the individual or group of users, and an idea of how those tools might be effectively organized. There should also be discussion and consensus on how time-sensitive the work page will need to be, and current awareness or new site announcements should be identified to keep the work page current.

The planning process should include the following considerations:

Who is using the home page? Will it be marketing, R&D, the newsroom, the students, the administrators, a combination of several departments? The answers to these questions will affect the search strategies and organization of the home page.

What is the mission of the organization? Profit, K–12 education, prize-winning journalism? The answers to these questions will affect the depth of knowledge one will need to cover, and how often the cybrarian updates the page.

What are the major areas of research in the organization? AIDS, grant proposals and awards, a unit on natural disasters for a science class? The answers here will give a cybrarian some ideas of useful keywords, and also how often the page will need to be updated.

A good first step in discerning what kinds of resources should be on the home page is to simply talk to the user base, or conduct a survey to find out what projects are of current interest and how often their information needs change.

Strategies for Gathering URLs

Search strategies are tactical plans for developing a collection of resources. Once you have discerned what the user is looking for, it is time to develop a strategy for gathering those materials. A typical library may incorporate several types of search strategies to cover all of the information needs of its user base.

Deciding how to search can be a very practical, or sometimes given, process. Many in-house developers report their sites have started from bookmark files kept on individual PCs.

From the information gathered in the planning process, a cybrarian should be able to answer the following questions:

- Are the users relying heavily on governmental data, press releases and news reports, grant awards and opportunities, or some other type of information?
- Is there a specific format of information that users want to collect, such as photos or software?
- What depth of information do the users tend to need? Do they want research reports from WAIS databases, or child-oriented sites?

Answering these kinds of questions will get at the nut of what information you need to search, and the next step is to translate that need into action—what Internet tools to use, for example. Another important component of the search strategy is to discern what print materials will supplement the Internet resources. For example, if there is a government office that is relevant to your organization, you would not only want to provide a link to the home page, but perhaps also provide some information on what documents can and cannot be found on the Internet.

Reviewing and Selecting

Before adding a URL to the home page, some process of verification and/or review should occur. At the very least, visit the site to assure that the address is accurate and that the content is appropriate. A conscientious cybrarian will look deeper than this, however, to find the specific link in a Web site that answers the information need and select that specific link for the home page. This will save the user's time by avoiding the hazard of getting lost browsing through needless layers of information. The Lycos search engine can aid the cybrarian in this process. Because the service catalogs every link in a Web site, the search results will often list several links from the same site, enabling the cybrarian to narrow down the meaningful link directly from the search results.

Critical reviews of Web sites are another way of finding and selecting URLs. These reviews consider readability, organization, and overall quality, and are becoming more available in print as well as from on-line sources. Lycos, once again, is an important aid to cybrarians, offering reviews with its search results. Lycos ranks its sites by popularity. It can also serve as a reviewing tool for cybrarians, as it suggests what other people are commonly referencing. OpenText's Power Search feature allows the cybrarian to use more complex operators and to search by fields.

Here are some other on-line review sources:

- Web Review
  http://www.gnn.com/gnn/wic/news.49.html

- The Atlas of the World Wide Web
  http://www.rhythm.com/~bpowell/Atlas/home.htm

- WebSight Magazine Online
  http://www.websight.com

There are other print resources that can be useful for finding and selecting URLs. Most Internet magazines as well as scholarly and trade publications will offer a column on Internet resources. Several other print publications list, describe, and review Web sites. Here are some examples:

- *The Wall Street Journal* publishes a section of advertising for businesses that have a presence on the Web.
- *The Internet Newsroom* newsletter features a regular column about Web sites that refer to news events and beats.
- *In Site* is a newsletter for information professionals.
- *The Internet Connection* is a newsletter of governmental information available on the Internet.

Organizing

After collecting the URLs, it's time to organize them on the home page. The primary consideration is what other materials will be on the home page, besides Web resources. In planning the layout of the home page, it may be useful to organize by the structure of the real-life office. *The Raleigh News & Observer*'s internal home page is one example of this real-life organization. Reporters there access the home page from any computer in the newsroom. Newsroom staff can also access the text and photo databases, and submit a research request through an e-mail link.

Other methods for organizing might include grouping resources for a specific project, or by the type of information—governmental, audio and photo files, general reference, and the like. A cybrarian might also word the index in such a way to entice users to try certain sites. Whenever possible, try to place the link in the context of the organization, and incorporate buzz words or keywords from a research topic. This can encourage new users to try a resource they haven't used yet.

Updating and Publishing

From the time the cybrarian starts organizing the home page, the job becomes more like publishing and editing than librarianship, and depending on the amount of text one includes with a link, a home page can walk a fine line between an on-line newsletter and a list of links. In a dynamic information and business environment, something like an in-house newsletter would be the ideal medium for presenting Internet information.

A more important factor, however, is the amount of time the cybrarian has to cull the Internet for new resources and update the home page. Most cybrarians are still working in their free time, or only after their other duties are finished. But keeping the home page meaningful can quickly encroach on one's time. Cybrarian Sperry Krueger reports that he spends about one day of work per week to keep up the *Raleigh News & Observer*'s in-house home page. Because of its new status in the workplace, cybrarians should prepare documentation to show how much time the job takes and what reorganization might be necessary to keep the office productive.

A Final Thought

Complaints of commercialization, chaos, and mediocre content on the Web only serve to underscore the need for content developers. With a careful audit of the users' information needs and collection development based on those needs, cybrarians can deliver the promise of a meaningful, powerful, and productive cyberspace. This outline introduces us to the issues facing cybrarians and provides a guideline for content development in a professional setting. For more detailed information and further insights, consult the following list of resources published in the last year:

Cronin, Mary J. *Doing Business on the Internet: How the Electronic Highway is Transforming American Companies.* New York: Van Nostrand Reinhold, 1994.

Levin, Jayne, et al. *The Federal Internet Source.* Washington, D.C.: National Journal Inc. and NetWeek L.L.C., 1995.

Peete, Gary R. *Business Resources on the Internet: A Hands-on Workshop.* Berkeley, California: Library Solutions Press, 1995.

Peete, Gary R. *Business Resources on the Internet Plus: A Hands-on Workshop.* Berkeley, California: Library Solutions Press, 1995.

Ryan, Joe. *Resources for Building and Managing Internet Services.* Syracuse, New York: Ryan Information Management, 1995.

St. Clair, Guy. *Customer Service in the Information Environment.* London, New Jersey: Bowker-Saur, 1993.

Tague-Sutcliffe, Jean. *Measuring Information: An Information Services Perspective.* San Diego: Academic Press, 1995.

Zimmerman, Donald E. *The Elements of Information Gathering: A Guide for Technical Communicators, Scientists, and Engineers.* Phoenix, Arizona: Oryx Press, 1995.

■

CHAPTER 9

Internet Publishing: A Beginner's Guide to Writing HTML

by Thomas Timmons

Hypertext Markup Language (HTML) is the "common tongue" of the World Wide Web. It allows anyone with the ability to create text documents and save them in "raw text" or ASCII format, to create Web pages. For anyone who was processing documents before the advent of graphical screen displays, HTML will look familiar. It is merely raw text, with formatting codes (or "tags") to tell the viewing software browsers how to organize the document. Currently, browsers are often configured to display actual pages differently, so HTML is a way of structuring a document, rather than a way of determining how it is displayed. Browsers often let the viewer customize how pages are displayed, including choosing colors and fonts for the various HTML tags. This, however, is in the process of changing.

In use since 1990, HTML has undergone a number of upgrades to increase its functionality—including in-line graphics and support for fill-in forms—and the improvements continue. One of the biggest changes in the works is to give the Web designer more control over how a document is actually displayed. This includes determining text colors as well as the ability to determine what fonts are to be displayed, use of text tables, background colors, text flow around images, and the like.

As of this writing, however, the current version of HTML is 2.0, and the commands to determine colors, fonts, and the like, have either yet to be officially released or are confined to a specific browser (such as Netscape 1.1x).

Although HTML version 3.2 (which addresses many of these capabilities) is in the works, I have chosen to confine my remarks to HTML 2.0 and certain commands that, while supported by only certain Web browsers, are coming into widespread use due to the popularity of the Netscape Web browser.

Browser-specific HTML commands are possible because Web browsers are designed to ignore any command that they do not understand. This allows, for example, a command to place an image onscreen to be enhanced with a command to size the image to specific dimensions. A browser that has not been programmed to understand the enhanced command will place the image onscreen in its actual dimensions. However, Web page designers must be careful to design pages for the widest possible audience—if a browser-specific command will render the page unintelligible for users of other browsers, a version of the page that uses only standard HTML commands should also be offered.

Writing Web Documents

Web documents, from the simplest text-only pages to the wildest multimedia experiences, are all based on the same basic HTML structure, a simple text document "marked-up" with formatting codes or tags. Although the complexity of HTML skyrocketed in 1995—the text file that describes how to create HTML 2.0 documents was seventy-one pages long, while the HTML 3.0 specification (the "work in progress" on the new version as of 1995) is 190 pages long—it is still possible to use a simple text editor to create interesting, design-rich pages for the Web using a small number of HTML tags.

How HTML Tags Are Structured

Tags are set off from regular text by the use of the less-than and greater-than signs, < and >. Since these data characters are used as part of the document formatting language, its is recommended that if you have a need in your text for one of these symbols, you use an "entity reference" or a "character reference." This eliminates the possibility that browser software will try to read your text as a tag. (The references for greater-than are &gt or &#62 and for less-than are &lt or &#60. Since the ampersand is also used in references, it is sometimes advisable to use &amp or &#38 to display an ampersand.) For more information on entity references, consult the list of HTML references later in this chapter.

Tags are usually structured like this:

<START-TAG NAME>Content of tag</END-TAG NAME>

For example, to put text in bold, you would use the "bold" tag:

<B>This text is bold</B>

Some tags do not currently have end-tags, such as LINE BREAK, PARAGRAPH, HORIZONTAL RULE, or LIST ITEM. However, the usage of these tags may change in the future. (See specific sections on these tags for more information.)

Types of Tags

Most HTML tags currently in use can be broken down into four simple categories:

1. Tags used to tell the browser that the file it is reading is an HTML document
2. Tags used to format text
3. Tags used to link the file with other files, actions, or other locations within the current file
4. Tags used to place images into the document

Presented below are the essential HTML tags that every Web designer should know. There are many more tags, and even more to

171

come in HTML 3.2, but the following will allow the novice Web designer to begin to stake out territory on the new electronic frontier. This list specifically excludes (due to their complexity or requirements for special arrangements with Internet providers) Fill-in Forms, Image Maps, Tables, and Gateway Scripts. For more information on these, consult the list of recommended sources at the end of this chapter.

Format of Tags

While much on the Internet is "case-sensitive"—i.e. the file TEST.TXT is not the same as Test.Txt—due to the UNIX operating system upon which much of the Internet is built, HTML itself is "case-insensitive." That is, the tag <TITLE></TITLE> is exactly the same as <title></title> and <TitLe></tItLE>. It is usually recommended, however, to place tags in ALL CAPS, to make it easier to work on your pages. HTML also ignores extra spaces and hard returns, making it useful to add extra hard returns to your document to separate the various sections of your page for easier editing. When extra returns are not added, it often becomes very difficult to determine where you are in the document. This is especially true with documents that have numerous links, text-formatting codes, images, or tables.

When a tag calls for the use of quotation marks, it is very important that *both* the opening and the closing quotes are used. Many browsers will return an error message or otherwise garble the page if the closing quote mark is omitted.

Tags That Must Be Used

HTML documents are made up of two areas: a "head" and a "body." The head area is the document's title, usage, and relationship with other documents (for advanced users), and the body is the area of main text and images that the user will see and interact with. Thus, all HTML documents must have the following four commands: "HTML," "HEAD," "TITLE," and "BODY." Note: Many browsers will allow you to omit the BODY command, but it is always recommended that you use all four of the "must-use" commands.

■ HTML Tag

- *Rationale:* Identifies the document as an HTML document.
- *Usage:* <HTML> begins the document, </HTML> ends it.
- *Special Instructions:* Within the HTML document, there must be a HEAD and a BODY tag. The HTML tags will be the first and last elements of any HTML document.

■ HEAD Tag

- *Rationale:* Provides the browser with information about the document
- *Usage:* <HEAD> begins the header area, </HEAD> ends it.
- *Special Instructions:* Within the HEAD tag, there must be a TITLE tag.

■ TITLE Tag

- *Rationale:* Used to identify the contents of the document. The title is usually displayed by the browser software in a title list or as a label for the window displaying the document.
- *Usage:* <TITLE> begins the title line, </TITLE> ends it.
- *Special Instructions:* Titles should be less than 64 characters long.

■ BODY Tag

- *Rationale:* Used to identify the text area of the document, including headings, paragraphs, lists, and images.
- *Usage:* <BODY> begins the body area, </BODY> ends it.
- *Special Instructions:* Netscape allows additional arguments within the BODY tag, which allow either a repeating graphic (either a GIF or a JPEG) to be used as a background pattern, or specific color to be selected for the background color, text color, and color of hypertext links. The same </BODY> end-tag is used.
- *Background Image:* <BODY BACKGROUND="filename.gif">.
- *Background Color:* <BODY BGCOLOR="FFFFFF"> where FFFFFF is the hexadecimal description of the color. (See list at end of chapter for the codes for a variety of colors.)
- *Text Color:* <BODY TEXT="FFFFFF">.

173

- *Highlight Color of a Hyperlink:* <BODY LINK="FFFFFF">.
- *Highlight Color of a Previously Used Hyperlink:* <BODY VLINK= "FFFFFF">.
- *Highlight Color of a Hyperlink When It Is Clicked:* <BODY ALINK= "FFFFFF">.

All of the color arguments can be included at the same time (in any order) within a single BODY tag.

Sample HTML Page:

```
<HTML>
<HEAD>
<TITLE>This is an HTML Document</TITLE>
</HEAD>
<BODY>
This is the main text of this document.
</BODY>
</HTML>
```

Text Formatting Tags

■ COMMENT Tag

- *Rationale:* While technically not a text tag, the comment tag is useful as a way to set various sections of the HTML page apart to ease the editing process.
- *Usage:* <!– begins the comment line, –> ends it.
- *Special Instructions:* Keep comment tags to a single line. If a longer comment is required, use two or more separate comment lines.

■ PARAGRAPH Tag

- *Rationale:* Sets apart text that is to be displayed as a single paragraph of standard text.
- *Usage:* <P> begins the paragraph, </P> ends it.
- *Special Instructions:* Currently, there is no requirement for a closing tag in the PARAGRAPH tag. So the tag acts as a spacer

between blocks of text. In the future, though, the PARAGRAPH tag should be able to determine alignment and spacing, and will require a closing tag. Thus, it is recommended to begin using the closing tag now.

■ HEADING Tag

- *Rationale:* Used for headlines, titles, or other short statements that are to be set apart from regular text.
- *Usage:* <H1> begins the heading area, </H1> ends it.
- *Special Instructions:* The heading tag accepts heading levels from 1 to 6, with decreasing emphasis.

■ CENTER Tag

- *Rationale:* This Netscape-specific tag allows a block of text, headline, table, or graphic to be centered within the screen of the viewer's browser.
- *Usage:* <CENTER> begins the heading area, </CENTER> ends it.
- *Special Instructions:* Be careful; if the closing tag is omitted, the entire document will be centered.

■ FONT Tag

- *Rationale:* This Netscape-specific tag allows text size to be specified as either larger or smaller point size than the default settings.
- *Usage:* <FONT SIZE=+X> begins the area of text to be modified, </FONT> ends it.
- *Special Instructions:* The example above would increase the default font size by X points. Using the following would decrease the font by 2 points: <FONT SIZE=–2> The FONT tag can be used in either PARAGRAPH or HEADING text.

■ BOLD Tag

- *Rationale:* To create boldface text.
- *Usage:* <B> begins the bold area, </B> ends it.

175

- *Special Instructions:* Another tag that serves much the same function is <STRONG>.

■ ITALICS Tag

- *Rationale:* To create italics.
- *Usage:* <I> begins the italics area, </I> ends it.
- *Special Instructions:* Bold and italics tags can be "nested" within each other to create bold italics. Other tags that serve much the same function as the italics tag are <ADDRESS> and <EM>.

■ HORIZONTAL RULE Tag

- *Rationale:* Creates a screen-wide ruling line.
- *Usage:* <HR> creates a horizontal rule.
- *Special Instructions:* There is no closing tag for a horizontal rule. Netscape-specific modifications to the HORIZONTAL RULE tag include: <HR SIZE=x>, where x equals the number of pixels high the line will be; <HR WIDTH=x%>, where x equals the percentage of the screen width the line will extend; and <HR ALIGN=LEFT>. The ALIGN comment also accepts CENTER and RIGHT arguments. All of these arguments can be used within a single HR tag.

■ LINE BREAK Tag

- *Rationale:* Forces an end to the current line of text.
- *Usage:*
 ends the current line of text.
- *Special Instructions:* There is no ending tag for a line break.

■ ORDERED LIST Tag

- *Rationale:* To create a hierarchically ordered list. Useful when the first item is the most important.
- *Usage:* <OL> begins the ordered list area, </OL> ends it.
- *Special Instructions:* Individual items have the LIST ITEM tag.
- *Example:*
  <P>To make a Hot Fudge Sundae, you need:</P>
  <OL>

```
<LI>Vanilla Ice Cream
<LI>Hot Fudge
<LI>Whipped Cream
<LI>A Cherry
</OL>
```

This would result in the following text appearing on the screen:

To make a Hot Fudge Sundae, you need:
1. Vanilla Ice Cream
2. Hot Fudge
3. Whipped Cream
4. A Cherry

■ UNORDERED LIST Tag

- *Rationale:* To create a bulleted list of items, without any hierarchical order.
- *Usage:* <UL> begins the ordered list, </UL> ends it.
- *Special Instructions:* Individual items have LIST ITEM tag.
- *Example:*
```
<P>To make a Hot Fudge Sundae, you need:</P>
<UL>
<LI>Vanilla Ice Cream
<LI>Hot Fudge
<LI>Whipped Cream
<LI>A Cherry
</UL>
```

This would result in the following text appearing on the screen:

To make a Hot Fudge Sundae, you need:
- Vanilla Ice Cream
- Hot Fudge
- Whipped Cream
- A Cherry

177

■ LIST ITEM Tag

- *Rationale:* Individual items in an ordered or unordered list.
- *Usage:* <LI> indicates a list item.
- *Special Instructions:* Individual list items do not currently require a closing tag, but future iterations of HTML may require it, so you may want to include a closing tag.

■ PRE Tag

- *Rationale:* Formats text as monospaced, Courier typeface.
- *Usage:* <PRE> begins the area of preformatted text, </PRE> ends it.
- *Special Instructions:* Useful for indicating that the are of text is typewritten or printed from a computer. Also maintains line breaks and spaces, making it possible to line up two or more columns of text without using tables. The typewriter text tag <TT> also uses Courier typeface, but does not read extra spaces and hard returns.
- *Example HTML Page With Text Formatting Features:*
  <HTML>
  <HEAD>
  <TITLE>This is an HTML Document With Text Formatting</TITLE>
  </HEAD>
  <BODY BGCOLOR="F5F5F5" TEXT="2F4F4F" LINK="00A6A6" VLINK="FF1493" ALINK="00BFFF">
  <!—This is a Comment line—>
  <H1>Usually Your First Line is a Heading</H1>
  <!—This is the main text area.—>
  <P>This is the main text of this document.</P>
  <P>This text <B>is in bold</B>, while this text <I>is in italics</I>. This text <B><I>is in bold italics</I></B>. Nested format tags should always follow the formula First In, Last Out. If the text is bolded first, then italicized, the italics should have its closing-tag before the bold closing-tag.</P>
  <PRE>This text is in monospaced Courier typeface.</PRE>
  <!—This is list area.—>
  <!—Extra hard returns do not show up when the page is viewed.—>

```
<!—You can put spaces in before the list items to make them
easier to read—>
<P>This is an unordered list:</P>
<UL>
<LI>Item One
<LI>Item Two
<LI>And So On . . .
</UL>
<HR><P>It is not necessary to put each tag on its own line, but
it is simpler to modify a file that has each tag on its own line,
with plenty of extra hard returns setting apart various sections.
<BR>HORIZONTAL RULES and LINE BREAKS are good at setting
apart areas of text</P>
<HR ALIGN=CENTER SIZE=5 WIDTH=50%>
<H2>Sometimes You Need Subheads In Your Document.</H2>
<P>This text is <FONT SIZE=+5>Really Big!</FONT></P>
<CENTER><P>Its often a good idea to put the date the file was
last updated at the end of your document so people will know
that they have hit the end of the page, as well as giving them
an idea of how current your site is.</P></CENTER>
<I>Today's Date</I>
</BODY>
</HTML>
```

Linking Tags

The linking or "anchor" tag <A></A> is often considered to be a single tag, with two specific purposes, first, to link to another file or place, and second, to set an anchor point for future linking. However, since the terms "link" and "anchor" describe two completely different actions, I am treating them as two tags.

■ ANCHOR Tag

- *Rationale:* The anchor tag allows the linking tag A HREF (see below) to be used to jump to a specific part of a remote document, or to navigate within the current document.

- *Usage:* <A NAME="EXAMPLE"> begins the anchor area, </A> ends it.

Special Instructions: Once an anchor has been set, the A HREF command may be used to direct the browser to that anchor. The text within the anchor area will *not* be highlighted.

■ LINKING Tag

- *Rationale:* Allows the current document to link to another file or to a specific place in a file. This is the feature around which the entire Web was constructed.
- *Usage:* <A HREF="file.name"> begins the hyperlink area, </A> ends it.
- *Special Instructions:* The text within the <A HREF></A> command will be highlighted with a special color (usually blue) to indicate that clicking on this text will take you to a different Web document. Since this command interacts with the rest of the Internet, the file name reference is case-sensitive. There are a number of ways of using the linking tag. Here are a few examples:

  Linking to a local document: <A HREF="file.NAME">text</A>

  Clicking on the highlighted word text will take you to the document named file.NAME, which is in the same directory as the current document.

  Linking to a remote document: <A HREF="http://www.test.com/file.NAME">text</A>

  Clicking on the highlighted word text will take you to the document named file.NAME, which is located at the Web address www.test.com.
- *Using File Transfer Protocol:* <A HREF="ftp://ftp.test.com/">text</A>. Clicking on the highlighted word text will take you to the File Transfer Protocol (FTP) server of the Internet domain test.com.
- *Using Gopher:* <A HREF="gopher://test.com/">text</A>. Clicking on the highlighted word text will take you to the Gopher site of the Internet domain test.com.
- *Sending Mail:* <A HREF="mailto:sample@test.com">text</A>. Clicking on the highlighted word text will send e-mail to the Internet address sample@test.com.
- *Reading Newsgroups:* <A HREF="news:name.of.group">text</A>.

Clicking on the highlighted word text will access the newsgroup name.of.group. (This feature is not supported on all browsers.)

- *Navigating Within a Document:* <A HREF="#EXAMPLE">text</A>. Clicking on the highlighted word text will take you to the place in the current document that has the anchor name EXAMPLE.
- *Linking to a Specific Place in Another Document:* <A HREF="file. name#EXAMPLE"> text</A>. Clicking on the highlighted word text will take you to the anchor <A NAME="EXAMPLE"> in the document named file.NAME, which is in the same directory as the current document.
- *Linking to a Specific Place in a Remote Document:* <A HREF="http:// www.test.com/file. NAME#EXAMPLE">text</A>. Clicking on the highlighted word text will take you to the anchor EXAMPLE in the document named file.NAME which is located at the Web address www.test.com.
- *Using an Image as a Hyperlink:* <A HREF="file.NAME"><IMG SRC="example.gif"></A>. Clicking on the highlighted image example.gif will take you to the document file.NAME. To indicate that it is a hyperlinked image, it will have a blue border surrounding it.
- *Sample HTML Page with Links:*
```
<HTML>
<HEAD>
<TITLE>This is an HTML Document With Links</TITLE>
</HEAD>
<BODY>
<!—Here is the Table of Contents—>
<P>The following are some uses of the A HREF tag:</P>
<A HREF="#LINK">Linking to Another File</A><BR>
<A HREF="#LINK_TO_REMOTE">Linking to a Remote File</A><BR>
<A HREF="#FTP">Using an FTP Link</A><BR>
<A HREF="#MAIL">Using an Mail Link</A><BR>
<A HREF="#GOPHER">Using a Gopher Link</A><BR>
<A HREF="#NEWS">Using a Usenet Link</A><BR>
<P>Click on any of the above to move to the section desired.</P>
<!—Here are the Subject Areas—>
<HR>
```

<A NAME="LINK">Linking to Another File</A>
<A HREF="anotherfile.html"> Clicking here</A> will take you to the file anotherfile.html.
<HR>
<A NAME="LINK_TO_REMOTE"> Linking to a Remote File</A>
<A HREF="http://www.anothersite.com/anotherfile.html"> Clicking here</A> will take you to the file anotherfile.html, located on the Web server of anothersite.com.
<HR>
<A NAME="FTP"> Linking to an FTP Server</A>
<A HREF="ftp://ftp.anothersite.com/anotherfile.exe"> Clicking here</A> will retrieve the file anotherfile.exe using the FTP server of anothersite.com.
<HR>
<A NAME="MAIL"> Using an E-mail Link</A>
<A HREF="mailto:myname@mysite.com"> Clicking here</A> will send mail from your browser to the e-mail address myname@ mysite.com.
<HR>
<A NAME="GOPHER"> Linking to a Gopher Server</A>
<A HREF="gopher://gopher.anothersite.com"> Clicking here</A> will allow you to browse the gopher server on anothersite.com.
<HR>
<A NAME="NEWS"> Linking to a Usenet Newsgroup</A>
<A HREF="news:name.of.group"> Clicking here</A> will allow you to browse the Usenet newsgroup name.of.group.
</BODY>
</HTML>

Image Placement Tag

■ IN-LINE IMAGE Tag

- *Rationale:* To place an image on your page.
- *Usage:* <IMG SRC="example.gif"> places a graphic on your screen.
- *Special Instructions:* While the GIF format has long been the most common image format on the Web, today most browsers will

accept either GIF or JPEG in-line images. Using the full Web address of a remote image can allow you to place an image stored on a remote Web server on your page. <IMG SRC="http://www.sitename.com/example.gif"> will place the image example.gif from the Web site www.sitename.com. Be sure to get permission before using other people's images. Additional arguments may be added between the IMG and the SRC in any order or combination. They include:

ALT Displays text on either browsers that cannot display in-line images, or on certain browsers prior to the download of the image. <IMG ALT="Text" SRC="example.gif"> The word Text will be displayed in the place where the image example.gif would normally be shown.

ALIGN The basic ALIGN commands, TOP, MIDDLE, and BOT-TOM, determine how the image aligns itself with the text it is adjacent to. Thus, the command <IMG ALIGN=TOP SRC="example.gif"> would align the top of the image example.gif with the top of the line of text. The Netscape-specific extension (although growing in support from other browsers) is the ALIGN=RIGHT, which places the image on the right-hand side of the screen, instead of the default of left-justification. <IMG ALIGN=RIGHT SRC="example.gif"> The image example.gif would be placed on the right-hand side of the screen. To center an image, nest the <IMG SRC> command within a <CENTER> command.

BORDER Netscape-specific command to determines the thickness of the hyperlink line surrounding the image. <IMG BORDER=x SRC="example.gif"> The image example.gif would have a border x pixels wide. A setting of 0 will eliminate the hyperlink border. This is useful if your GIF file has a transparent background and a big blue square around the image would harm the overall design of the page.

HEIGHT/WIDTH Netscape-specific command to determines the dimensions of the image. <IMG HEIGHT=x WIDTH=y SRC=

"example.gif"> The image example.gif would be displayed as x pixels high and y pixels wide. This is useful when an image is larger than you desire for your page. Making an image too small, however, sometimes eliminates the transparent background on some GIF files.

Sample HTML Page With Images:

```
<HTML>
<HEAD>
<TITLE>This is an HTML Document With Images</TITLE>
</HEAD>
<BODY>
<IMG SRC="example.gif">Here is a standard image. It is left-justified, and the text will flow from the bottom left-hand corner of the image.
<IMG ALIGN=RIGHT SRC="example.gif">In Netscape, this image will be right-justified. Text will begin on the next line.
<CENTER><IMG SRC="example.gif">Here is a centered image.
<BR>This text will also be centered.</CENTER>
<A HREF="newfile.html"><IMG SRC="example.gif"></A>Here is an image used as a link to the file newfile.html.
<A HREF="newfile.html"><IMG BORDER=0 SRC="example.gif"></A>Here is the same image used as a link to the same file, but with no distinctive "hyperlink" border.
</BODY>
<HTML>
```

HTML Coded Character Set

The following is from the HTML 2.0 specification, by Tim Berners-Lee and Daniel Connolly, August, 8, 1995.

This list details the code positions and characters of the HTML document character set, specified in 9.5, "SGML Declaration for HTML."

REFERENCE	DESCRIPTION
&#00; – &#08;	Unused
&#09;	Horizontal tab
&#10;	Line feed
&#11; – 	Unused
&#13;	Carriage Return
&#14; – &#31;	Unused
&#32;	Space
&#33;	Exclamation mark
&#34;	Quotation mark
&#35;	Number sign
&#36;	Dollar sign
&#37;	Percent sign
&#38;	Ampersand
&#39;	Apostrophe
&#40;	Left parenthesis
&#41;	Right parenthesis
&#42;	Asterisk
&#43;	Plus sign
&#44;	Comma
&#45;	Hyphen
&#46;	Period (full stop)
&#47;	Solidus (slash)
0 – 9	Digits 0–9
&#58;	Colon
&#59;	Semicolon
&#60;	Less than
&#61;	Equals sign
&#62;	Greater than
&#63;	Question mark
&#64;	Commercial at
A – Z	A–Z (upper case)
&#91;	Left square bracket
&#92;	Reverse solidus (\)
&#93;	Right square bracket
&#94;	Caret
&#95;	Horizontal bar (_)
&#96;	Acute accent
a – z	a–z (lower case)
&#123;	Left curly brace
&#124	Vertical bar
&#125;	Right curly brace
&#126;	Tilde (~)
&#127; – Ÿ	Unused
	Non-breaking space
&#161;	Inverted exclamation
&#162;	Cent sign
&#163;	Pound sterling
&#164;	General currency sign
&#165;	Yen sign
&#166;	Broken vertical bar
&#167;	Section sign
&#168;	Umlaut (dieresis)
&#169;	Copyright
&#170;	Feminine ordinal
&#171;	Left angle quote, left guillemets
&#172;	Not sign
&#173;	Soft hyphen
&#174;	Registered trademark
&#175;	Macron accent
&#176;	Degree sign
&#177;	Plus or minus
&#178;	Superscript two
&#179;	Superscript three
&#180;	Acute accent
&#181;	Micro sign
&#182;	Paragraph sign
&#183;	Middle dot
&#184;	Cedilla
&#185;	Superscript one
&#186;	Masculine ordinal
&#187;	Right angle quote, right guillemets

&#188;	Fraction one-fourth	&#210;	Capital O, grave accent
&#189;	Fraction one-half	&#211;	Capital O, acute accent
&#190;	Fraction three-fourths	&#212;	Capital O, circumflex accent
&#191;	Inverted question mark	&#213;	Capital O, tilde
&#192;	Capital A, grave accent	&#214;	Capital O, dieresis or umlaut mark
&#193;	Capital A, acute accent	&#215;	Multiply sign
&#194;	Capital A, circumflex accent	&#216;	Capital O, slash
&#195;	Capital A, tilde	&#217;	Capital U, grave accent
&#196;	Capital A, dieresis or umlaut mark	&#218;	Capital U, acute accent
&#197;	Capital A, ring	&#219;	Capital U, circumflex accent
&#198;	Capital AE diphthong (ligature)	&#220;	Capital U, dieresis or umlaut mark
&#199;	Capital C, cedilla	&#221;	Capital Y, acute accent
&#200;	Capital E, grave accent	&#222;	Capital THORN, Icelandic
&#201;	Capital E, acute accent	&#223;	Small sharp s, German (sz ligature)
&#202;	Capital E, circumflex accent	&#224;	Small a, grave accent
&#203;	Capital E, dieresis or umlaut mark	&#225;	Small a, acute accent
&#204;	Capital I, grave accent	&#226;	Small a, circumflex accent
&#205;	Capital I, acute accent	&#227;	Small a, tilde
&#206;	Capital I, circumflex accent	&#228;	Small a, dieresis or umlaut mark
&#207;	Capital I, dieresis or umlaut mark	&#229;	Small a, ring
&#208;	Capital Eth, Icelandic	&#230;	Small ae diphthong (ligature)
&#209;	Capital N, tilde		

186

&#231;	Small c, cedilla		&#244;	Small o, circumflex accent
&#232;	Small e, grave accent		&#245;	Small o, tilde
&#233;	Small e, acute accent		&#246;	Small o, dieresis or umlaut mark
&#234;	Small e, circumflex accent		&#247;	Division sign
			&#248;	Small o, slash
&#235;	Small e, dieresis or umlaut mark		&#249;	Small u, grave accent
&#236;	Small i, grave accent		&#250;	Small u, acute accent
&#237;	Small i, acute accent		&#251;	Small u, circumflex accent
&#238;	Small i, circumflex accent		&#252;	Small u, dieresis or umlaut mark
&#239;	Small i, dieresis or umlaut mark		&#253;	Small y, acute accent
&#240;	Small eth, Icelandic		&#254;	Small thorn, Icelandic
&#241;	Small n, tilde			
&#242;	Small o, grave accent		&#255;	Small y, dieresis or umlaut mark
&#243;	Small o, acute accent			

Hexadecimal Color Codes

The following is list of hexadecimal codes for various colors. The hexadecimal code is used in the Netscape-specific BODY command to determine the page background color, the font color, and the color of hyperlinked text. Note: Do not put spaces between the numbers in the BODY command.

Hex Code	Color			
			00 00 00	Black
FA EB D7	Antique white		FF EB CD	Blanched almond
32 BF C1	Aquamarine		00 00 FF	Blue
F0 FF FF	Azure		8A 2B E2	Blue-violet
F5 F5 DC	Beige		A5 2A 2A	Brown

DE B8 87	Burlywood	7C FC 00	Lawn green
5F 92 9E	Cadet blue	FF FA CD	Lemon
7F FF00	Chartreuse	B0 E2 FF	Light blue
D2 69 1E	Chocolate	F0 80 80	Light coral
FF D6 56	Coral	E0 FF FF	Light cyan
22 22 98	Cornflower blue	EE DD 82	Light goldenrod
FF F8 DC	Cornsilk	A8 A8 A8	Light gray
00 FF FF	Cyan	FF B6 C1	Light pink
00 56 2D	Dark green	FF A0 7A	Light salmon
BD B7 6B	Dark khaki	20 B2 AA	Light sea green
55 56 2F	Dark olive green	87 CE FA	Light sky blue
FF 8C 00	Dark orange	84 70 FF	Light slate blue
E9 96 7A	Dark salmon	7C 98 D3	Light steel blue
8F BC 8F	Dark sea green	FF FF E0	Light yellow
38 4B 66	Dark slate blue	00 AF 14	Lime green
2F 4F 4F	Dark slate gray	FA F0 E6	Linen
00 A6 A6	Dark turquoise	FF 00 FF	Magenta
94 00 D3	Dark violet	8F 00 52	Maroon
FF 14 93	Deep pink	00 93 8F	Medium aquamarine
00 BF FF	Deep sky blue		
8E 23 23	Firebrick	32 32 CC	Medium blue
FF FA F0	Floral white	32 81 4B	Medium forest green
50 9F 69	Forest green		
F8 F8 FF	Ghost white	D1 C1 66	Medium goldenrod
DA AA 00	Gold	BD 52 BD	Medium orchid
EF DF 84	Goldenrod	93 70 DB	Medium purple
33 33 33	Gray 1	34 77 66	Medium sea green
66 66 66	Gray 2	6A 6A 8D	Medium slate blue
99 99 99	Gray 3	23 8E 23	Medium spring green
CC CC CC	Gray 4		
00 FF 00	Green	00 D2 D2	Medium turquoise
AD FF 2F	Green yellow	D5 20 79	Medium violet red
F0 FF F0	Honeydew	2F 2F 64	Midnight blue
FF 69 B4	Hot pink	F5 FF FA	Mint
6B 39 39	Indian red	FF E4 E1	Misty rose
FF FF F0	Ivory	FF E4 B5	Moccasin
B3 B3 7E	Khaki	FF DE AD	Navajo white
E6 E6 FA	Lavender	23 23 75	Navy blue

FD F5 E6	Old lace	52 95 84	Seagreen
6B 8E 23	Olive	FF F5 EE	Seashell
FF 87 00	Orange	96 52 2D	Sienna
FF 45 00	Orange red	72 9F FF	Sky blue
EF 84 EF	Orchid	7E 88 AB	Slate blue
EE E8 AA	Pale goldenrod	70 80 90	Slate gray
73 DE 78	Pale green	FF FA FA	Snow
AF EE EE	Pale turquoise	41 AC 41	Spring green
DB 70 93	Pale violet red	54 70 AA	Steel blue
FF DA B9	Peach	DE B8 87	Tan
FF B5 C5	Pink	D8 BF D8	Thistle
C5 48 98	Plum	FF 63 47	Tomato
B0 E0 E6	Powder blue	19 CC DF	Turquoise
A0 20 F0	Purple	9C 3E CE	Violet
FF 00 00	Red	F5 DE B3	Wheat
41 68 E1	Royal blue	FF FF FF	White
8B 45 13	Saddle brown	F5 F5 F5	White smoke
E9 96 7A	Salmon	FF FF 00	Yellow
F4 A4 60	Sandy brown	32 D8 56	Yellow green

Recommended Sources

Lemay, Laura. *Teach Yourself Web Publishing with HTML in a Week.* Indianapolis: SAMS Publishing, 1995.

net.Genesis and Hall, Devron. *Build a Web Site.* Rocklin, CA: Prima Publishing, 1995.

Heslop, Brent and Budnick, Larry. *HTML Publishing on the Internet.* Chapel Hill: Ventana Press, 1995 (Includes CD-ROM Online Companion).

■

Glossary

To help the novice navigate the unfamiliar waters of the Internet, we have compiled a list of essential, informative, and amusing terms common to global networking.

Before we begin in alphabetical order, let's start with the word Internet.

Internet The common name for a global collection of inter-linked computer networks all using the same communication protocol (see TCP/IP). Commonly known as the Net.

A Must-Know Net Glossary

Archie, Veronica, WAIS The two characters from the famous *Archie* cartoon series and the Wide Area Information Server are all various tools for finding information and files on the Net.

ARPAnet The Internet's direct ancestor. It began operation in 1969 with money from the Defense Department's Advanced Projects Research Agency.

ASCII (American Standard Code Information Interchange) Knowing about ASCII, or at least that it exists, is handy for sending text over the Internet in some cases. This is the de facto worldwide standard for the code numbers that are employed by computers to designate all upper and lower case Latin letters, numbers, punctuation, and other characters.

backbone This is the high-speed line or set of connections that are the major framework for data transmission within a network. The Internet, being a network of networks, uses a variety of backbones maintained by different organizations, both academic and commercial.

bandwidth The "bandwidth" of your Internet connection determines how much data can be sent over the line. Standard copper wire telephone connections are the lowest bandwidth and fiberoptics the highest. Also: The capacity to transmit or absorb information. Used to describe both computer systems and people. Low-bandwidth folks can be easily spotted by the flashing "12:00" on their VCRs.

baud The baud rate of a modem is commonly understood to mean how many bits-per-second it can transmit.

bit (*binary digit*) The bit is a single number in base-2, which means it is either a one (1) or a zero (0). The bit is also the smallest unit of computerized data.

bps (bits per second) This is the measurement of data speed from one computer location to another. I.E. a 28,800 modem moves can move data at a rate of 28,800 bits-per-second.

browser The chief "client" software used for using the Internet, a Browser allows you to "read" the material—text, graphics—that is on the World Wide Web. Currently the most popular Browser in usage is Netscape Navigator.

Clipper Chip A government-sponsored plan for telecommunications encryption. While signals would automatically be encrypted, the Feds would keep a master list of decryption keys.

cyberspace The environment that exists within a global computer network and the place where discussion, news and events happen in the on-line world. Coined by William Gibson in his 1984 novel *Neuromancer*, the term has spawned new suffixes and prefixes—cyberpunks and Gopherspace to name a few.

e-mail Electronic mail. A form of asynchronous communication on the Internet and other networks—i.e. the recipient does not have to be on-line at the time the message is sent. Also used as a remote information distribution system—"an e-mail server."

FAQ Frequently Asked Questions. A list of these questions, posted regularly in Usenet newsgroups and in the ftp site rfm.mit.edu, seek to answer questions for new Internet users before they are asked. Reading the FAQ is a good way to avoid getting flamed.

Finger This is an Internet function that allows users to locate persons on the Net. Specifically you use the Finger to see if someone has an account at any particular domain on the Net.

flame To yell at someone or otherwise criticize them on-line. Flaming e-mail is often distinguished by the use of CAPITAL LETTERS AND EXCLAMATION MARKS!!!

FTP File Transfer Protocol. This is a method for moving files—particularly large ones—between computers that involves using the Internet to log onto another computer from your own and access its FTP directory for publicly available files that you can then transfer back to your computer. FTP files can be anything from an entire book to free software files.

gateway This the technical term for the computer setup that translates material using dissimilar communication protocols. Most often this term is used in reference to the "gateway" between one of the big on-line services—i.e. America Online, CompuServe, etc.—and the Internet-at-large.

Gopher This aptly named rodent "client" utility is the best way to negotiate the Net if you have a text-based connection. It enables you to browse through a large series of interconnected menus.

GIF Stands for Graphics Interchange Format. The most common type of image file found on the Net. Limited to 256 colors, it is gradually being supplanted by the 24-bit Joint Photographic Experts Group (JPEG) compression format, which allows smaller file sizes.

host These are the computers on the Internet that act as the repository for services that can be used by other computers connecting to the host. Also, the host computer is where a "home page" is geographically situated and can be located.

HTTP This stands for *H*yper*t*ext *T*ransport *P*rotocol, a.k.a. Hypertext Transfer Protocal, which is the protocol whereby the Web works, using "Hypertext" links that act to connect files across the entire Internet.

I.P. number Every machine that is on the Net has a specific I.P. or Internet Protocol number to identify it and help route transmissions to and from that site.

IRC Internet Relay Chat. The IRC is essentially a large-scale "chat" function of the Internet that allows multi-users to all converse via messages in realtime.

ISDN Integrated Services Digital Network.

mail bomb The punishment of choice for serious violators of the rules of behavior of the Usenet. A mail bomb is a huge e-mail message that clogs a perpetrator's host system. When hundreds of mail bombs deluge a system, it can cause a computer to crash. Similarly, a fax bomb sends an endless sheet of black paper to the victim's fax machine, consuming the paper supply or burning out the machine.

Mosaic This is software for navigating the World Wide Web. You can reach the WWW if you have a graphics-based Internet connection. A windows-type program, Mosaic is pretty cool-looking. There is a commercial version, but Mosaic can be downloaded free from numerous Internet locations and BBS.

Netiquette The unofficial "Rules of Etiquette" of the Internet. Small violations often result in flaming, while more serious offenses risk incurring a mail bomb attack.

Net god An oldtimer in the Net world. One who remembers when the Net was only two computers and a piece of string.

Netsurfer One who cruises the waves of the Net perpetually looking for new spots to get their feet wet. Also, used a term for connecting to the Net just for the thrill of exploration. Often referred to as simply "surfing."

newbie A Net newcomer. A negative term used by old-timers who resent the use of resources by an ever-expanding population of network novices. Most common usage as in "clueless newbie."

spamming To send out multiple non-germane postings on the Usenet. To post messages that have nothing to do with the affected newsgroups is a cardinal Net sin. The response can be severe (see *mail bomb*).

Slip/PPP Serial Line Internet Protocol and Point-to-Point Protocol are one of the several methods for connecting directly to the Net over the phone.

Telnet A way of tapping into a remote computer—as if directly connected—in order to access its publicly-available files.

TCP/IP Transmission Control Protocol/Internet Protocol is the shared language of all computers on the Net.

World Wide Web (a.k.a. WWW) The is most organized facet of the Net by virtue of a series of interconnected "pages" which include text, graphics, sound, and video.

■

Index

Allworth Books

Allworth Press publishes quality books to help individuals and small businesses. Titles include:

The Internet Publicity Guide by V. A. Shiva
(softcover, 6 × 9, 208 pages, $18.95)

Arts and the Internet: A Guide to the Revolution by V. A. Shiva
(softcover, 6 × 9, 208 pages, $18.95)

The Business of Multimedia by Nina Schuyler
(softcover, 6 × 9, 240 pages, $19.95)

The Photographer's Internet Handbook by Joe Farace
(softcover, 6 × 9, 208 pages, $18.95)

The Writer's Internet Handbook by Timothy K. Maloy
(softcover, 6 × 9, 208 pages, $18.95)

Mastering the Business of Writing by Richard Curtis
(softcover, 6 × 9, 256 pages, $18.95)

The Writer's Legal Guide by Tad Crawford and Tony Lyons
(softcover, 6 × 9, 304 pages, $19.95)

Business and Legal Forms for Authors and Self-Publishers
Revised Edition by Tad Crawford (softcover, 8½ × 11, 192 pages, $19.95)

Writing Scripts Hollywood Will Love by Katherine Atwell Herbert
(softcover, 6 × 9, 160 pages, $12.95)

Electronic Design and Publishing: Business Practices
Revised Edition by Liane Sebastian (softcover, 6¾ × 10, 216 pages, $19.95)

The Copyright Guide: A Friendly Handbook for Protecting and Profiting from Copyrights by Lee Wilson
(softcover, 6 × 9, 192 pages, $18.95)

Please write to request our free catalog. If you wish to order a book, send your check or money order to Allworth Press, 10 East 23rd Street, Suite 400, New York, NY 10010. Include $5 for shipping and handling for the first book ordered and $1 for each additional book. Ten dollars plus $1 for each additional book if ordering from Canada. New York State residents must add sales tax.

If you wish to see our catalog on the World Wide Web, you can find us at Millennium Production's Art and Technology Web site:

http://www.arts-online.com/allworth/home.html

or at **http://www.interport.net/~allworth**